What
Jesus
Taught

Interpretive essays on
Key Issues Addressed by
the Lord Jesus Christ

by
William L. Owens

Published by
The 222 Plan Ministries
610 Republican Road
Clarks Hill, SC 29821

Printed in the USA
by CreateSpace, North Charleston, SC
United States of America
an Amazon Company

ISBN-13: 978-1517698096
(CreateSpace-Assigned)
ISBN-10: 151769809X
BISAC: Religion / Biblical Studies / Jesus/ Gospels

Biblical text quoted from the
King James Version

Acknowledgements

I am more than appreciative for the hours my friends have spent to make this writing project presentable to the public. These friends include the Reverend Richard Daniels, his wife Sue, and my friend Dianne Casey. They participated in proofreading, making suggestions, and encouraging me.

I am also grateful for the Bible teachers God has brought into my life. The truths they have shared have become so much a part of me that I often do not know to whom credit should be given.

Some of my teachers and spiritual heroes (either in life or literature) are: John Bunyan; W. A. Criswell; Lewis S. Chafer; Charles Campbell; M. R. DeHann; Francis W. Dixon; Charles Hodge; Vance Havner; Jesse Penn-Lewis; L. E. Maxwell; J. Vernon McGee; John MacArthur; Stephen Olford; Ruth Paxson; A. W. Pink; Lenard Ravenhill; Adrian Rodgers; Erich Sauer; Bertha Smith; Charles Haddon Spurgeon; R. C. Sproul; Miles Stanford, Cornelius Van Til; Robert G. Witty and others whom have made an impact on my life and ministry.

Dedication:

To the Faithful Members of

The Bible Class

at Rolling Green Village

Greenville, SC

WHAT JESUS TAUGHT

FOREWORD

Dr. William L. Owens is an exceptional teacher, preacher, communicator, and practitioner of the Word of God.

In his recent publication, What Jesus Taught, Dr. Owens gives to the serious student of the Bible a strong revelation of the major theological and doctrinal issues Jesus treated in His ministry among mankind.

Dr. Owens, using the parables, miracles, sermons, and prayers of our Lord, gives to the reader basic lessons on such subjects as the Trinity, Satan, temptation, eternal life, abundant living, discipleship, hell, heaven, and end times. Through compassionate, heart-felt pastoral exposition, interpretation, and application, he opens the teachings of Jesus to mind and heart.

What Jesus Taught is a valuable tool to be used in small groups, seminars, Sunday School classes, or individual pursuit of a deeper understanding of our Lord's declarations.

I was exceedingly blessed by the integrity, depth, and wisdom inherent in this writing; and, I commend it as a "must" study for the genuine student of God's Word.

Dr. Robert B. Whaley,
December 21, 2015

INITIAL CONSIDERATIONS

In the fall of 2004, I was impressed with the thought that I should begin a winter/spring preaching series focusing on the Gospels. As I considered the idea, it occurred to me that the sermons should center on what Jesus taught about eternal issues for which people need answers. Jesus' teachings are applicable for every century including the twenty-first.

I began the series in January of 2005. The congregation seemed responsive to the presentations and some expressed their delight to contemplate what Jesus had taught as a unique focus. Therefore, I offer these brief essays for spiritual contemplation and enrichment. It is my wish that you study the topics prayerfully with a genuine desire to alter your personal life by listening to God's voice and obeying Him.

The teachings of Christ were never presented as an ethical system to be mimicked. But, rather as a window through which the believer may gain a glimpse of the Father's true character. Having seen His character, and left to our own devices, we are then confronted with the utter impossibility of becoming like Him. Jesus taught us, through these life issues, that we are totally dependent upon His grace. We will never successfully live the Christian life without His supernatural power working in us.

God's Spirit will lead you into a discovery of His truth. My prayer is that your quest for knowledge will lead you to worship and praise our Lord Jesus Christ. I have found through more than five decades of preaching His Gospel that our sole purpose is to glorify the Son of God so that the Son may glorify the Father.

As you read, please keep in mind the presuppositions addressed in the thoughts that follow.

Challenge everything written by man (including me). Study the Scriptures to make sure what you read is what the Scriptures teach. There are times when an author or speaker may inform you that his conclusions are his own opinions. In this case, take it under advisement until the Holy Spirit confirms it in the Word.

The topics in this little volume are independent interpretive essays concerning the teaching of our Lord. We are limiting our consideration to the four Gospel writings— only here do we have a record of the actual words of Christ. While the subjects are not to be considered exhaustive, every attempt is made to treat each subject thoroughly within the confines of the gospel accounts.

We have confidence that nothing Jesus taught in these historical gospels is contradicted in any other portion of God's Word. A basic principle of interpreting the Bible contends that an absolute meaning for a text is found when its interpretation is consistent with the meaning of other biblical texts addressing the same issue. Therefore, we interpret Scripture with Scripture.

My personal conviction is that the Bible is inerrant (without error) in the original autographs (Greek, Aramaic and Hebrew manuscripts). My confidence is held for three basic reasons; (1) the Bible itself claims divine authorship; (2) copies of the manuscripts have survived extraordinary circumstances to the end that there is more evidence for its claims than any other book of antiquity; (3) the evidence of the men used in writing the manuscripts overwhelmingly points to them as being men of integrity. Most gave their lives for maintaining what they witnessed to be true and they all endured relentless persecution without wavering in their faith.

My main concern is that we understand clearly what Jesus taught about each topic and that we make applicable personal application to our daily lives. However, one must remember that Christ's ministry was primarily to the Hebrews. Therefore, be careful to discern what was applicable only to Israel and what is transcultural for all believers.

Without your personal commitment, you will not understand His truth nor become His disciple. You can only gain from these messages if you are committed to Christ. Otherwise, it will be an exercise in futility.

I have deliberately chosen to use the King James Version. Why? Because its Elizabethan style is different enough from our casual English to cause us to stay focused as we read and ponder its meaning. Should you be troubled by not understanding its word usage, I suggest you consult a good dictionary. You will find that the translators have chosen their words well in turning the original writing into an English translation.

I suggest you begin each reading with prayer. Ask God for guidance in the discovery of His truth. Just because you can read and are intelligent, does not mean that you will have an automatic understanding of God's truth. God, the Holy Spirit, must illumine truth or you will never have insight beyond what may be comprehended historically, geographically, and culturally.

Reading just for the sake of getting information is an exciting exercise and reading brings a real sense of satisfaction when your research bears fruit. However, a biblical study is intended by God to be more than an intellectual rush or even an emotional and spiritual high. He intends to effect a change in (1) your heart (2) your will and (3) ultimately your life.

Remember, Scripture has only one meaning but may have many applications as directed by the Holy Spirit. My prayer for you, the reader, is that God will reveal Himself to you and give you a discerning spirit so you will know the distinction between interpretation and application.

My prayer is that His grace will attend your reading as you think about His truth.

William L. Owens

CONTENTS

Chapter 1
  What Jesus Taught: Historical Background   15
Chapter 2
  What Jesus Taught: About God The Father   23
Chapter 3
  What Jesus Taught: About The Son of God   45
Chapter 4
  What Jesus Taught: About The Holy Spirit   59
Chapter 5
  What Jesus Taught :   AboutThe Devil   75
Chapter 6
  What Jesus Taught: About Temptation   91
Chapter 7
  What Jesus Taught: About Eternal Life   107
Chapter 8
  What Jesus Taught: About Abundant Living   125
Chapter 9
  What Jesus Taught: About Discipleship   145
Chapter 10
  What Jesus Taught: About Hell   159
Chapter 11
  What Jesus Taught: About Heaven   173
Chapter 12
  What Jesus Taught: About The End Times   191
Appendix I
  Parables of Jesus   211
Appendix II
  Miracles of Jesus   215

CHAPTER 1

HISTORICAL BACKGROUND TO WHAT JESUS TAUGHT

In the beginning God created everything including our first parents Adam and Eve. Nothing exists that God did not create!

In Genesis 3 we are informed of the prohibition placed on Adam and Eve. After God had breathed into them the **breath of life**, He placed them in the garden—in a district called Eden. Adam was given the charge to care for the earth and Eve was to be his helpmate.

In Eden flowed a river that had trees along its shores that bore life sustaining fruit. Only one prohibition was given them by their creator. They were not to eat of the tree *in the midst of the garden*. For if they should eat of it they would lose God's gift of eternal life. They would immediately be under the curse of death. They would immediately die spiritually and physical death would eventually follow.

Adam and Eve were tested by Satan who appeared to them as a beautiful serpent. He deceived Eve into eating of the forbidden tree by convincing her that God really did not mean what He said. Adam, though not deceived, also ate from the tree. They immediately died spiritually. Spiritual death is separation from God (the source of life). From that initial experience of yielding to temptation, man has been in need of being rescued from his state of spiritual death. With separation from God comes the sentence of eternal punishment.

Therefore, salvation, as referenced in the Bible, is restoration from sin or eternal death. The entrance of sin brought God's judgment. God judged sin by placing a curse upon the whole creation. It appears that only the faithful angels and God's dwelling place were exempted.

Because of Adam and Eve's disobedience, God pronounced a curse on (1) Satan (the tempter and adversary), (2) Adam and Eve, (3) and the planet (It likely included all physical creation with the exception of God's home). Remember, the curse was pronounced because our first parents ate fruit from the **forbidden tree** (Genesis 3). Therefore, all who are born of the first parents inherit their sin nature and are also condemned by the curse—separated from God and in a state of spiritual death.

The whole human race is under the curse of God's judgment. As alluded to above, every person existing after Adam and Eve inherit their sin nature. That means each one of us has an inbred tendency to be drawn to self-centeredness, selfishness, and self-glory. In this condition, it is natural for us to seek fulfillment of our own desires without concern for the will of God.

The curse upon mankind is alienation from God and is man's inheritance. Unless God does something to make a way for restoration (to provide a way to return to God's favor) we remain lost. All humanity is like a broad, mighty river rushing to the fires of eternal judgment—a judgment God prepared for Satan and his fallen angels (Matthew 25:41).

God in His mercy and grace provided coverings of skins for Adam and Eve. These coverings were a sign of restoration to God and His fellowship. This is significant because, in eating the forbidden fruit they had lost their sense of innocence. They had become ashamed of their nakedness; their fellowship with God was broken. Their awareness of nakedness was the fruit of their rebellion in disobeying God.

When they received the skins for coverings, their fellowship with God was restored. This restoration of fellowship was all the work of the Father. Metaphorically speaking, Adam and Eve did not lift one finger of assistance in their own behalf nor could they. In themselves, they had no power to change their sinful condition. They could not undo their sin! They were truly recipients of mercy and grace. Once fellowship was restored, their hearts were filled with love and a desire to obey and please Him. In providing skins, God revealed a hint at the means He would use to save all who in faith will come to Him.

Many theologians believe that in order for God to be justified in providing the animal skins, a plan had to be in place that satisfied both His justice and His mercy. Such a plan would have had to be in place before the foundations of the world. Why? Because, God's holiness will not allow Him to tolerate sin.

Sin did not take God by surprise! In eternity past, before man's history began, the Son of God gave His assent to be the Lamb of God slain as a substitute for the sin of the world (all God's creation). Therefore, in the **mind of God**, Jesus was the blood sacrifice for all sin before the world was even created. Why? Because the decree regarding Christ's crucifixion had already been given, God was justified in forgiving all whom in faith would **believe Him** (Romans 4:3).

Why would God need justification to forgive men their sins? If God is God, can He not do anything He wishes? No!

There is one thing that God cannot do; He cannot violate His own character. God is Holy! Sin is a rebellion against His character. Holiness cannot allow unrighteousness to exist in its presence; therefore, God must exterminate the rebellion. Neither can God excuse sin. To excuse something is to overlook it or pretend it did not happen. God cannot do that! He cannot receive sin into His presence. Sin deserves judgment for what it is, a violation of His pristine holiness! It must be eliminated!

Therefore, He cannot receive or accept man into His presence because man is a sinner. In order for God to grant forgiveness, one who is innocent must be willing to pay for these sins. A sinful man does not qualify to offer payment for his own sin—he is not holy. An innocent one who is holy must pay. The Lord Jesus agreed to do that. (God gave His promise and sealed it even before sin had invaded God's creation.)

As history unfolded, the provision of animal skins to cover Adam and Eve was the first of many revealing hints that God has provided. For example, He gave His people the Levitical system of blood sacrifices through Moses. The sacrificial system pointed to the ultimate sacrifice of God's Son for the sins of the world. God's people believed, and their faith was evidenced by their obedience. Because of their faith, God graciously justified them on the grounds of the Son's shed blood before the foundation of the world (Revelation 13:8).

In the days our Lord was ministering on the earth, the way of salvation was not properly understood. Knowledge seemed to be limited to the fact that the Messiah would come as the deliverer. The evidence indicates that no one expected the Messiah to die for the sins of man. Even His disciples could not accept the fact that He must die—that He came to die. The expectation of Judaism was that the Messiah would establish the prophesied kingdom and restore Israel's glory to the days of David and Solomon. Those Jews who still reject Jesus Christ still look for the Messiah.

God's ultimate goal is to restore glory to Himself through the destruction of evil and the eternal punishment of Satan, his demons, and all who love sin.

Study Guide

1. What did God forbid Adam and Eve to do?

2. Who tempted them to disobey God?

3. How did the tempter deceive Eve?

4. What is the penalty for disobeying God?

5. Read Genesis 3 and list those persons and things that were cursed and why.

6. What provision did God make for Adam and Eve to cover their nakedness?

CHAPTER 2

WHAT JESUS TAUGHT:ABOUT THE FATHER

Those of us who are trinitarian believe God is one God (Deuteronomy 6:4). However, we discern from Scripture that God shows Himself to us in three personalities. These three are all equally God and are generally referred to by Bible teachers as forming the God-head. The God-head is composed of three persons. The first person is God the Father. Jesus Christ, the Son of God, is the second person. The Holy Spirit, the Spirit of God, is the third person.

While each person of the trinitarian God-head is equally God, each one fulfills a function that is uniquely His own. Allow me to use an illustration to show how the persons of the God-head function. Remember, human illustrations are not perfect and will often fail to adequately communicate the spiritual principle being illustrated. With that understanding, lets proceed. It appears to me that the Father functions as the God-head's visionary and policy maker. God the Son functions as the executor of the Father's policies, and God the Spirit provides the power whereby the policies become reality. We may safely conclude that Jesus did not do or think outside the will of His Father. On one occasion He said: . . .*what I see my Father do, I do.* He also said: *I and My Father are one.* His level of commitment to His Father was absolute!

The key to understanding what Jesus taught about His Father lies in our observing how Christ responded to Him. When we gain insight into the Son's relationship to His Father, we then will know how the Father relates to us.

The Father desired that Jesus follow Him. Jesus learned as He followed. We often forget that Jesus was human while also being fully divine. He was God incarnate in flesh. He was just as truly human as He was divine. I do not pretend to know how to explain this mystery, but I also cannot deny that its precept is taught throughout the Gospels as well as the Pastoral and General Epistles of The New Testament.

To say that Jesus was human means that He went through the developmental stages of human life. He experienced infancy as a baby—He became a young man—with all its emotional and physical limitations. He then grew into an adult who fulfilled a threefold office of Prophet, Priest, and King. Every phase of His life had its natural human characteristics of growth, pain, discomfort, joy, ecstasy, and sorrow. While He had every human emotion, yet He did not express Himself or act outside the will of His Father. Not once, in all His experiences of life, did He commit sin (Sin is acting or thinking contrary to the will of God, the Father).

It was as if, for the sake of His mission, He laid aside His divine attributes and willfully left the glory of His Father's home. While in human flesh, His divine attributes were shrouded by the very flesh He inhabited. It was as if He chose to lay aside the public display of His divinity for the sake of rescuing man and the entire universe from the dreadful condition of being in bondage to sin.

Consider now what Jesus taught about His Father.

Jesus Taught That His Father Desires Glory

What is glory? Glory—from the human side—is exaltation and praise. True believers are those who worship Jehovah through Jesus Christ in the power of the Holy Spirit. Worship is glorifying God through praise and exaltation of His person and character. We praise God for whom He is! In Matthew 5:13-16 Jesus said:

> *Matthew 5:13-16*
> *13 Ye are the salt of the earth: but if the salt have lost his savour, wherewith shall it be salted? it is thenceforth good for nothing, but to be cast out, and to be trodden under foot of men*
> *14 Ye are the light of the world. A city that is set on an hill cannot be hid.*
> *15 Neither do men light a candle, and put it under a bushel, but on a candlestick; and it giveth light unto all that are in the house.*
> *16 Let your light so shine before men, that they may see your good works, and glorify your Father which is in heaven.*

Here, Jesus tells the parable of **salt and light**. It is obvious to the most casual reader that Jesus is describing the purpose God has for believers in the world. Salt retards corruption and provides flavor for what our bodies consume. Light provides sight in the midst of darkness. Therefore, believers should simply be who we are. Christians are the salt of the earth and the light of the world.

In being what we are, salt and light, we become a witness to the way of God. We influence our world by our very presence. Our just being here retards the power of evil and provides light to those around us. People watch us and we influence them just as salt retards corruption in meat and light drives away darkness. The Lord loves to see His people living as He has instructed them. Why? Because, your faith-filled life brings *glory* to His name in the midst of spiritual corruption and darkness.

Worship and exaltation of God blesses Him and brings much joy to Him. But, such worship is only acceptable when your heart has the proper motive. When Jesus taught that God desires glory, He was not teaching us that God was an ego-maniac. Our heavenly Father is worthy of our praise and worship. For Him, to desire such praise from you is the natural fulfillment of His purpose in creating you. You are who you are because you are born again and are now a part of a spiritual family. As a member of His family, you have certain spiritual characteristics. These characteristics now are seen in your life. Your acts of goodness and kindness will be seen by the world and will bring glory to our heavenly Father. It is the glory He receives from your life of willing obedience that brings Him the most pleasure.

Obedience is required if we are to be salt and light. And yet, consistent obedience is impossible without a faithful daily walk disciplined by prayer and communion in the Scriptures. Therefore, by God's grace walk with Him that you may glorify Him.

Jesus Taught That
His Father Blesses All Mankind

God is a benevolent God. He blesses all of mankind. This is what Jesus said in:

> *Matthew 5:43-48*
> *"43 Ye have heard that it hath been said, Thou shalt love thy neighbour, and hate thine enemy.*
> *44 But I say unto you, Love your enemies, bless them that curse you, do good to them that hate you, and pray for them which despitefully use you, and persecute you;*
> *45 That ye may be the children of your Father which is in heaven: for he maketh his sun to rise on the evil and on the good, and sendeth rain on the just and on the unjust.*
> *46 For if ye love them which love you, what reward have ye? do not even the publicans the same?*
> *47 And if ye salute your brethren only, what do ye more than others? do not even the publicans so?*
> *48 Be ye therefore perfect, even as your Father which is in heaven is perfect."*

The above passage was spoken primarily to Israel. It is likely that the Lord was painting a picture of His high ethical standard expected of the true household of God. Those listening were incapable of obeying the instruction. Actually, no one, except Christ Himself, can follow these instructions perfectly. Jesus' teaching in this passage fo-

27

cuses on how life would be lived if one were filled with and obeyed the Holy Spirit.

Remember, the Holy Spirit had not, yet, been given to indwell the hearts of men. That could not happen until after the crucifixion, burial, resurrection, and ascension of Christ. Only after Christ's ascension was the Spirit sent to fill the hearts of believers. Up to that time the Spirit came upon men to enable and empower them but He never indwelled them.

Now that the Spirit has come to indwell us, He will guide us through life's trials. He will give us a different attitude toward our neighbors and enemies. This love command of Jesus is impossible for us without divine empowerment. Which one of you finds it a natural emotion to love your enemy? Honesty demands that we want our enemy treated in a way that would put them down and exalt us. But that is not what Jesus commanded. That attitude is not the desire of our Father.

As Christians, we have indwelling us the presence of the Holy Spirit. He is God's divine enabler. What is impossible for you is quite easy for Him. Therefore, following the lead of the Spirit, we will be enabled to pray for the spiritual success and physical well-being of the one who may hate us. Most likely, our difficulty with what Jesus taught is our misuse of the word "love." Love is not an emotion. Love is action.

However, I ask you to focus on another concept in His teaching. Look carefully at verse 45: *for he maketh his sun to rise on the evil and on the good, and sendeth rain on the just and on the unjust.*

Here, Jesus teaches us that His Father provides a common grace of blessing to all mankind. He uses sunshine and rain as illustrations. When God shares the riches of His creation,

He does so in such a manner that all people benefit from the blessings.

When the rain falls, God does not act as a traffic cop directing rain to the righteous and withholding it from the wicked. He allows the falling rain to bless all people. When He provided air to sustain life, He did not choose to bless the righteous only but all mankind. However, it seems to me that only the thoughtful Christian truly gives God thanksgiving for these common graces.

Our Lord is calling our attention to the graciousness of His Father in providing blessings to all men. God is truly no respecter of persons. He also extends to all men an invitation to receive Jesus Christ as the Way, the Truth, and the Life. He chooses to withhold the blessings of saving grace from those who choose to reject the witness of His Spirit. Truly, God blesses all mankind.

Jesus Taught :
His Father Answers Prayer

Turn your attention to Matthew 6:5-15:

Matthew 6:5-15
5 And when thou prayest, thou shalt not be as the hypocrites are: for they love to pray standing in the synagogues and in the corners of the streets, that they may be seen of men. Verily I say unto you, They have their reward
6 But thou, when thou prayest, enter into thy closet, and when thou hast shut thy door, pray to thy

Father which is in secret; and thy Father which seeth in secret shall reward thee openly.

7 But when ye pray, use not vain repetitions, as the heathen do: for they think that they shall be heard for their much speaking

8 Be not ye therefore like unto them: for your Father knoweth what things ye have need of, before ye ask him.

9 After this manner therefore pray ye: Our Father which art in heaven, Hallowed be thy name.

10 Thy kingdom come. Thy will be done in earth, as it is in heaven.

11 Give us this day our daily bread.

12 And forgive us our debts, as we forgive our debtors.

13 And lead us not into temptation, but deliver us from evil: For thine is the kingdom, and the power, and the glory, for ever. Amen.

14 For if ye forgive men their trespasses, your heavenly Father will also forgive you:

15 But if ye forgive not men their trespasses, neither will your Father forgive your trespasses.

16 Moreover when ye fast, be not, as the hypocrites, of a sad countenance: for they disfigure their faces, that they may appear unto men to fast. Verily I say unto you, They have their reward.

17 But thou, when thou fastest, anoint thine head, and wash thy face;

18 That thou appear not unto men to fast, but unto thy Father which is in secret: and thy Father, which seeth in secret, shall reward thee openly.

Jesus taught His disciples that prayer is essential to sustaining a relationship with the Father. He set before them the **model prayer** and proceeded to instruct them in the auxiliary disciplines of fasting and privacy in personal worship. You do not worship God in a vacuum. Neither do you worship and petition Him in vain. God will always honor worship offered in **truth and Spirit**.

In Jesus' model prayer (sometimes called the Lord's Prayer) He provides us with an outline of how one's prayers should be practiced. Let us contemplate it phrase by phrase:

Our Father – He teaches us to honor the Father by acknowledging our relationship to Him and dependence upon Him. He is our Father because He has given us a spiritual birth through Christ His Son. As our Father, He is our total sustainer; He meets our every need.

which art in heaven, – We are not to lose sight of eternity. Our Father is in heaven. Therefore, we should desire to be where our beloved God is. Prayer is the key to our realization of eternity. Why? Because every time we pray we renew our awareness of eternity and its reality.

Hallowed be thy name – God's name is Holy. We are not coming into the presence of one that we can manipulate with our cunning or whining. He knows us and He cannot be fooled. We are free to be ourselves in His presence, and in His presence, we are in the presence of Holiness and Truth. He is so hallowed that we dare not enter with a known sin staining our life. Before coming into God's presence, sin must be confessed and forgiven ... then and only then ... will the Spirit allow us to approach His throne in full fellowship. (Perhaps this is the problem when we pray and feel we have not been heard.)

Thy kingdom come. – The world we live in is not our home. We are not to be preoccupied with the world's glamor and glitter. We are to live for the coming Kingdom whose capital is a city not made with hands—a Kingdom not of this world. The Master of that coming Kingdom is the Lord Jesus Christ and the desire of every Christian is fulfilled in that Kingdom.

Thy will be done in earth, as it is in heaven. – The will of God will someday rule supreme. Believers are surely the ones who will most benefit from this mastery of heaven and earth. We are both motivated and challenged to obey God because in doing so we express our faith that His sovereignty will be exercised on earth.

Give us this day our daily bread. – The people of God must never forget that our Father supplies all our human needs both spiritually and physically. It is fitting that we acknowledge Him as our sustainer. Our request for His supply shows our dependence upon Him.

And forgive us our debts, as we forgive our debtors. – Here, Jesus leads His people to confess their need for His forgiveness for specific sins. He also leads us to commit ourselves to the practice of forgiving those who wrong us just as God forgives our wronging Him.

And lead us not into temptation, but deliver us from evil: – The Epistle of James reminds us that God does not tempt man. However, He allows Satan to tempt us as a means of testing us. The distinction in temptation and testing is motive. One who tempts desires to overcome and destroy the one tempted, while one who tests does so for building up, and strengthening the one tested. Satan tempts us. Our Father tests us. Why does He test us? Perhaps, so we may know ourselves and thereby understand where we need to be strengthened. He knows us, but we often do not know ourselves.

For thine is the kingdom, and the power, and the glory, forever. Amen. Worship is an integral part of prayer. In fact, it is the ultimate goal of prayer.

He will always respond, if your motive is pure, and you are following His instructions. He promised not to leave you nor forsake you (Hebrews 13:5). The promise was originally given in Deuteronomy and repeated in Joshua. His promises (of a spiritual nature) are transcultural. Therefore, as the **bride of Christ**, we are able to claim the promise as well. He keeps His promises! He always answers the prayers of His children (John 1:12). His standard for responding to us is His sovereign will. God's will is always the best for those who are called by His name (Romans 8: 28, 29).

Jesus Taught:
His Father Reveals Himself

Matthew 11:25-27;
25 At that time Jesus answered and said, I thank thee, O Father, Lord of heaven and earth, because thou hast hid these things from the wise and prudent, and hast revealed them unto babes.
26 Even so, Father: for so it seemed good in thy sight.

*27 All things are delivered unto me of my Father:
and no man knoweth the Son, but the Father; neither knoweth any man the Father, save the Son,
and he to whomsoever the Son will reveal him.*

From the above passage, we glean several interesting things about when God reveals Himself to man. First, we learn in verse twenty-five that it is not God's will to reveal all things to all people. He hides spiritual truths from those who think themselves to be wise. He reveals the same to those who are like children. We learn from this that men must not presume to be worthy of having God invest His truth in them. If this passage says anything, it speaks of the sovereignty of God in spiritual revelation. God reveals Himself to whom He will.

In His humanity, even Jesus depended on the Father's reveling to Him things He needed to know as He needed to know them. Although Christ was fully God and therefore had access to all knowledge, He chose to limit Himself in keeping with the Father's will. The Father has willed that all things be delivered to the Son and that only the Father knows the Son. He also says that it is impossible for anyone to know the Father except those to whom Christ reveals Him.

Taking the above passage at face value, we must find a way to harmonize the Word of God with itself. In a general way apparently God wants us to know of His reality and has therefore given two witnesses: (1) the conscience and (2) physical creation. The conscience gives man light from birth (John 1:8, 9). He has also provided a witness to every person who can see the reality of the world's creation and its symmetrical order. In this way, our gracious

34

God has shown Himself to the entire world of mankind. Ultimately, He reveals Himself through His Son (John 1:9).

Consider another passage that will help us understand how God reveals Himself.

> *Matthew 16:17*
> *17 And Jesus answered and said unto him,*
> *Blessed art thou, Simon Bar-jona: for flesh and*
> *blood hath not revealed it unto thee, but my Father*
> *which is in heaven.*

In the context of this verse, we have the Lord Jesus asking Peter about who men were saying He was. Peter gave several responses of which he had become aware. Then Jesus asked Peter directly—Who do you say that I am? Peter's response was that Jesus was the Son of the living God. Upon hearing this, Jesus informs Peter that the source of his answer came not from his own observation but rather from God Himself.

Verse seventeen reinforces two things: (1) that the Father alone reveals His Son and that the Son cannot be known apart from the Father revealing Him; (2) a person cannot know God by any means apart from God opening his spiritual eyes. Man's pursuit of God is futile unless God in His mercy gives him an awareness of His reality and points him to His Son.

God has given all mankind an inner light of conscience and an outer light of creation. The witness of these lights takes away any excuse man may have for claiming he does not know right from wrong. The witness of these two lights, when responded to positively, will lead to the ultimate light who is Jesus the light of the world.

Look at yet another verse that provides more light on God revealing Himself.

> *John 6:65*
> *65 And he said, Therefore said I unto you, that no man can come unto me, except it were given unto him of my Father.*

The above verse was part of Jesus' teaching that His disciples were totally dependent upon Him. For example, earlier in the passage He had shared that those who were to have eternal life, must eat of His body and drink of His blood. Here, in the timeline of Jesus' life, those listening to Him were absolutely mortified that they were being asked to eat His body and drink His blood. They would later learn that he was speaking metaphorically. It was a literal statement to be taken as a metaphor.

You may well ask: How does this verse relate to the Father revealing Himself? Follow the contextual progression: (1) Jesus informs His followers that they must partake of Him (metaphorically eat His Body and drink His blood); (2) He informs them that partaking of Him will provide them with eternal life; (3) He informs them also that it will not be possible for them to partake of Him if the Father does not draw them.

Notice the phrase ". . .no man can come unto me, except it were given unto him of my Father." It is from this phrase that we perceive the Father revealing Himself. Here, we see that if anyone is to believe on Christ, the Father must give the spiritual ability to see who Jesus is and faith to believe on Him. Nothing could be clearer from the lips of our Lord but that His Father alone can provide the gift of eternal life and that He only gives that life to those whom He draws to the Son.

I can hear someone objecting! But, you say, cannot anyone who desires to believe on Christ do so? Yes, but I remind you, even your desire is the Father revealing His Son to you. Rejoice! He has been pleased to draw many to the Son.

Jesus Taught: the Father Desires Worship

Turn your thoughts to worship. The Lord Jesus had some key things to say about worshipping the Father.

> *John 4:21-24*
> *21 Jesus saith unto her, Woman, believe me, the hour cometh, when ye shall neither in this mountain, nor yet at Jerusalem, worship the Father.*
> *22 Ye worship ye know not what: we know what we worship: for salvation is of the Jews.*
> *23 But the hour cometh, and now is, when the true worshippers shall worship the Father in spirit and in truth: for the Father seeketh such to worship him. 24 God is a Spirit: and they that worship him must worship him in spirit and in truth.*

The above passage has as its central theme an interview with a woman whom the Lord met at Jacob's well. He had asked her for water to drink. His request led to a rather remarkable discussion about spiritual water that only He could provide. It was of such a nature that if one drank it, he would never thirst again. When received, His "water of life" will provide everlasting satisfaction to the soul.

The woman asks for the Lord to give her this water. She is intrigued by not needing to come again to the well. The conversation quickly turns to an interesting request. Jesus asks her to call for her husband. Here, she admits that she has no husband.

The Lord commends her for being truthful. For in reality, the man she was presently living with was not her husband. Not only that, she had actually had five husbands. She was startled and responded by saying: "Sir, I perceive You are a prophet." On the heels of the statement, she introduces the subject of worshipping God. She informs the Lord that the Samaritans worship on "This" mountain (Mt. Gerizim) while you Jews say that you should worship in Jerusalem (Mt. Moriah).

After her remark about worship, the Lord Jesus introduces a precious truth that had not been explained before. He informs her that both Samaritans and Jews are in error about true worship. He boldly says that the day will come when neither Mt. Gerizim or Mt. Moriah will be the place for worship. He teaches her and us that it is not about place but rather in what manner one worships.

With the arrival of Jesus, a new understanding of worship and its nature unfolds. True worship has always been personal. But, worship has never been explained this way before. What our Lord was teaching this woman was that worship, if not done in the manner dictated by the Father, is null and void.

What kind of worship did Jesus say the Father was seeking? He is seeking worshippers who will worship Him in truth and spirit. Therefore, clearly the worship of God must be based on truth and spirit. God is spirit, and He may only be worshipped in one's spirit. It is not about place but rather the attitude of your spirit. Do not forget the element called truth. God is to be worshipped within the environment of His truth. God must be worshipped and loved for whom He reveals Himself to be. As the Father reveals Himself through His Word, His children will find their spirits agreeing with His truth and will approach Him on the basis of His truth. We must receive His truth and agree before we may experience worship. One cannot be received in worship while in a state of rebellion. The Father desires only worshippers who are at one with His truth and in communion with His Spirit.

Jesus Taught:
He is One with the Father

John 5:16-30
16 And therefore did the Jews persecute Jesus, and sought to slay him, because he had done these things on the sabbath day.
17 But Jesus answered them, My Father worketh hitherto, and I work.
18 Therefore the Jews sought the more to kill him, because he not only had broken the sabbath, but said also that God was his Father, making himself equal with God.
19 Then answered Jesus and said unto them, Verily, verily, I say unto you, The Son can do nothing of himself, but what he seeth the Father do: for what things soever he doeth, these also doeth the Son likewise.

20 For the Father loveth the Son, and sheweth him all things that himself doeth: and he will shew him greater works than these, that ye may marvel.

21 For as the Father raiseth up the dead, and quickeneth them; even so the Son quickeneth whom he will.

22 For the Father judgeth no man, but hath committed all judgment unto the Son:

23 That all men should honour the Son, even as they honour the Father. He that honoureth not the Son honoureth not the Father which hath sent him.

24 Verily, verily, I say unto you, He that heareth my word, and believeth on him that sent me, hath everlasting life, and shall not come into condemnation; but is passed from death unto life.

25 Verily, verily, I say unto you, The hour is coming, and now is, when the dead shall hear the voice of the Son of God: and they that hear shall live.

26 For as the Father hath life in himself; so hath he given to the Son to have life in himself;

27 And hath given him authority to execute judgment also, because he is the Son of man.

28 Marvel not at this: for the hour is coming, in the which all that are in the graves shall hear his voice,

29 And shall come forth; they that have done good, unto the resurrection of life; and they that have done evil, unto the resurrection of damnation.

> *30 I can of mine own self do nothing: as I hear, I judge: and my judgment is just; because I seek not mine own will, but the will of the Father which hath sent me.*

In the passage above the Lord Jesus proclaims Himself to be at one with the Father in at least seven different ways:

1. In verse eighteen the Jews sought to kill Him because He claimed to be the Son of God. Such a declaration made Jesus equal to God, and therefore He was at one with Him.

2. The nineteenth and twentieth verses record the Lord Jesus being so in communion with the Father that He mirrored the Father's actions. His love for the Father and His Father's love for Him was such that what He saw His Father do, He did! Oh! If only our own hearts would develop that kind of sensitivity to the Father.

3. In verse twenty-two the Father shows His oneness with the Son by committing all judgment to the Son. Think about it! All judgments that man and angels face will be before the Son of God who has the mind of God, which is at one with God and will exercise the perfect blend of wrath and mercy as shown by God.

4. Verse twenty-three reports that the Father is so in union with the Son that He bestows all Honor to the Son. Their oneness is such that to honor the Father is to honor the Son, and to honor the Son is to honor the Father.

41

5. In verse twenty-four the Father reveals His oneness with the Son in yet another way. The Lord Jesus says that the one who believes on the Father who sent Him, has everlasting life. The oneness, of the Father and the Son, is illustrated in the fact that one who believes on the Father also believes on the Son.

6. The Father is the essence of life and in verses twenty-five through twenty-nine, He extends His **life** source to His Son. Christ's oneness with the Father is seen in His power to give life. We see the principle of oneness with the Father amplified in John 1:12 where Christ gives the **life** of the Father to all who receive the Son.

7. In verse thirty the Lord Jesus declares Himself to be impotent without the Father. Their oneness is seen in the fact that the Son is powerless to do the Father's will apart from the Father's power. The thought extends itself by God enabling us to see that with the Son's exercise of the Father's will comes an infusion of power. That power is in essence His **life** giving source.

These seven witnesses to the oneness of the Father and the Son provides us with greater insight into the Trinity of the God-head. It is readily perceived that the oneness of the Father, and the Son is accomplished by the communion of the Spirit who is the third person of the Trinity.

Study Guide

The Lord has been gracious to provide, through the Scriptures, insight into what Christ taught about God the Father. Therefore, as a review of the material, answer the following questions.

1) What is the **glory** desired by the Father?

2) How does the Father bless all mankind?

3) Why is the prayer recorded in Matthew 6 referred to as the model prayer?

4) Why does the Father reveal Himself?

5) What is the essence of worship?

6.) In what way did the Father show His oneness with the Son?

CHAPTER 3

WHAT JESUS TAUGHT:
About the Son

When the disciples were first called by Jesus, it is unlikely they were aware of Jesus' identity.

John's gospel begins with these words, "In the beginning was the Word, and the Word was with God, and the Word was God."

Jesus Taught:
The Son of God Is Truly Man

Two thousand years ago, Jesus referred to Himself as **Son of Man**. He said, in Matthew 8:20, "The foxes have holes, and the birds of the air *have* nests; but the Son of man hath not where to lay *his* head." In this statement, He identified Himself with all mankind. He who had ever been with the Father, was one with the Father in essence and nature. This Jesus who existed before time began, humbled Himself and became a man (John 1:1, 14).

When He came to earth He was born just as other children are born (Luke 2:4-7). His conception had been miraculous, but His birth was natural in every respect. There was nothing strange or extraordinary—no pomp and ceremony. Only the shepherds who had been made aware by the angels, and the few who had paid attention to prophecy, such as the wise men from the East, were even conscious of such an astounding event.

The priests of Judaism were unaware of Jesus' birth. His neighbors in Bethlehem nor those in Egypt where He and His parents had fled His attempted murder by King Herod knew anything of His royalty. Those who knew Mary and Joseph treated them as if they were common people, in a common world, doing common things.

He grew in wisdom and stature (Luke 2:40, 52). He was subject to the laws of human development in both body and soul (Luke 2:46). Mary and Joseph knew that their Son was the Son of God. There is no evidence that they had any information about how God would reveal Him to the world, unless, Mary had been given some clue when visiting Elizabeth--who had been pregnant with John (the Baptist).

It is also evident that His parents did not seek the council of the temple's leadership or any other religious leaders. They simply waited on God. They knew that at the right time all that was to be would unfold.

After Herod's death, an angel of the Lord informed them that they should return to their homeland. Being warned of God in a dream not to settle in Jerusalem, they continued northward to the Galilean district where they settled in the village of Nazareth. It was in the loving and caring climate of a carpenter's home that Jesus would spend his childhood. He grew as other children grew. He laughed, He cried, and He experienced the full range of human emotions but He did not sin.

There is little in the Gospels about His life before He entered upon His mission to become the sacrificial lamb of God. It is suspected that even Jesus was not fully cognizant that He was God incarnate until His visit to the temple when He became of age. In the early Jewish culture, a young man entered a new stage of maturity at age twelve. It was at such an age that Jesus' wisdom surprised the teachers of the Law in the synagogue. Their amazement was based on their observation of Jesus' maturity and spiritual wisdom in understanding the Scriptures.

As He grew in age, He also grew in spiritual and emotional maturity. As He moved among men in the affairs of life, He spoke like a man and looked like a man (Mark 15:34; Luke 24:32; John 4:9; John 20:15 and John 21:4-5). He was subject to the frailties of human nature (apart from sin). Contemplate the following physical conditions He experienced: (1) hunger (Matthew 4:2; Mark 11:12; John 19:28), (2) weariness (Mark 4:38; John 4:6), (3) pain (John 19:3; 28-30), (4) temptation (Luke 4:13); and (5) death (John 19:30).

He was the perfect Man and the only man who has ever lived without experiencing sin (Luke 23:41, 47; John 8:46; 19:4). He was, and is, truly Man. He completed His mission by becoming a sacrifice for all sin. Albeit, He allowed death to claim Him for the sake of mankind; He has risen again in a perfect human body proving Himself to be

47

victorious over sin and death (Matthew 28:6; Luke 24:13-34; John 20:14-16; John 21:1-14).

Upon His resurrection, He physically ascended with His humanity into the very throne room of God (Acts 1:9-11; 1Timothy 2:5; Hebrews 9:24). This Jesus is indeed the *man* Christ Jesus; as man He could enter the presence of God because He had no sin.

Jesus Taught:
The Son of God is Truly God

John 1:1-14
1 In the beginning was the Word, and the Word was with God, and the Word was God.
2 The same was in the beginning with God.
3 All things were made by him; and without him was not any thing made that was made.
4 In him was life; and the life was the light of men.
5 And the light shineth in darkness; and the darkness comprehended it not.
6 There was a man sent from God, whose name was John.
7 The same came for a witness, to bear witness of the Light, that all men through him might believe.
8 He was not that Light, but was sent to bear witness of that Light.
9 That was the true Light, which lighteth every man that cometh into the world.
10 He was in the world, and the world was made by him, and the world knew him not.

11 He came unto his own, and his own received him not.

12 But as many as received him, to them gave he power to become the sons of God, even to them that believe on his name:

13 Which were born, not of blood, nor of the will of the flesh, nor of the will of man, but of God.

14 And the Word was made flesh, and dwelt among us, (and we beheld his glory, the glory as of the only begotten of the Father,) full of grace and truth.

Notice in verse one of the text that Jesus is called the **Word**. The Greek philosophers, whom some think were the most erudite of all, believed the God that had the first original thought was superior to all gods. Because they could not identify who this god was, they erected a monument to the Unknown God and worshipped him least they offend him. It was in this environment that Paul, when preaching on Mars Hill, addressed the Greek philosophers. He commended them for being religious and sought to introduce them to the Unknown God. So John, when writing His Gospel ninety years later, uses "Word" to show that Jesus is identified with the God of original thought. He is showing that Jesus is not only a man, but truly God wrapped in human flesh.

It is quite commonly taught in twenty-first century academic circles that Jesus never claimed to be God. However, that is not true! Jesus did teach that He was truly God! He did not become God. He was God in eternity past, where He fellowshipped with His Father and enjoyed the glory of being God with the Father and the Spirit (John 1:1).

In the fulness of time, the Father sent Jesus to become our redeemer. In obedience to His Father, Jesus became a man and suffered for our sin. By completing His mission, Jesus enables the Father to forgive all who will come to Him on the basis of Christ's death (Galatians 4:4). He died that we may not die!

Jesus was always God, one with the Father and the Spirit (Colossians 2:9).

Compare John 1:1 with Matthew 1:23:

> *John 1:1*
> *1 In the beginning was the Word, and the Word was with God, and the Word was God.*
> *Matthew 1:23*
> *23 Behold, a virgin shall be with child, and shall bring forth a son, and they shall call his name Emmanuel, which being interpreted is, God with us.*

John reminds us that Jesus was always God and has therefore always existed. Matthew shows us that God in the person of Jesus is with us. The child was born, the Son was given. (The Son ever was the Son, but at Bethlehem the Son was given as a child—Luke 1:35.)

Repeatedly in The New Testament He is spoken of, by Himself and by others, as the Son of God (Matthew 3:17; 27:40-43; Mark 14:61-62; Luke 22:70; John 5:25; 10:36 and 11:4).

The Scriptures use the term—**the only begotten Son** (John 1:14, 18, and 3:16). This phrase means that God has only one son. There are no others! Someone might object and say, "But Christians are called sons of God." That is true, but we were **not begotten** we were **adopted** by the Spirit into God's family through the spiritual process called the **new birth**.

In John 1:12, 13 John said,

> *John 1:12, 13*
> *12 But as many as received him, to them gave he power to become the sons of God, even to them that believe on his name:*
> *13 Which were born, not of blood, nor of the will of the flesh, nor of the will of man, but of God.*

Receiving Christ means committing yourself to Him. Upon committing yourself to Christ, through faith in His sacrificial death for you, the Holy Spirit supernaturally adopts you into the family of God. When you experience this, Jesus becomes your elder brother and you are joint heirs with Christ (Romans 8:17).

At Caesarea Philippi Jesus commended Peter's confession that He was the Christ the Son of the living God. Jesus went on to say that Peter's testimony would become the foundation on which His Church would be built (Matthew 16:13-17). Jesus reminded Peter that he could only know who He was by God's witness to his heart. If we accept the witness of the Scriptures, we cannot deny that Jesus taught He was indeed the Son of God.

Turn your thoughts to the **I AM** passages found in John's Gospel. These Scriptures identify what Jesus said about Himself. **I Am** is the name God told Moses to use when asked about who sent him to lead Israel out of Egypt. Therefore, I Am is the name for God that speaks of

His eternal nature. He has no beginning. He is and has forever been.

Look at what Jesus said in John 6:35.

> *John 6:35*
> *35 And Jesus said unto them, I am the bread of life: he that cometh to me shall never hunger; and he that believeth on me shall never thirst.*

Jesus is claiming deity for Himself by making the promise to satisfy eternally the spiritual thirst and hunger of those who come to Him. My own conviction is that Jesus is not promising that believers will never experience physical hunger or thirst. He could have promised that, and He showed on several occasions that He could make a physical promise. However, that would not have been the will of the Father. Why? Because, God sometimes uses the adversities of life to develop His children (Romans 8:28).

> *John 8:12*
> *12 Then spake Jesus again unto them, saying, I am the light of the world: he that followeth me shall not walk in darkness, but shall have the light of life.*

Jesus is claiming to be the source of both **life** and **light**. In making such a claim He draws attention to His deity. The apostle John said that Jesus is the light that lights every man who comes into the world (John 1:9). He also stated in the Bible's last book that Jesus would be the light of the heavenly city (Revelation 21:23).

Three other I Am passages follow:

John 10:9
9 I am the door: by me if any man enter in, he
shall be saved, and shall go in and out, and find
pasture.
John 10:14
14 I am the good shepherd, and know my sheep,
and am known of mine.
John 14:6
6 Jesus saith unto him, I am the way, the truth, and
the life: no man cometh unto the Father, but by me.

Only God can claim to be the entrance into eternal life. In the three I Am's presented above Jesus uses the analogy of the shepherd's pastoral life in caring for the sheep. Not only is He the only entrance into heaven, only those who know His voice and follow Him will be in His fold. There is only one way to God, and only those who desire to come as Jesus has said will be admitted.

John 11:25, 26
25 Jesus said unto her, I am the resurrection, and
the life: he that believeth in me, though he were
dead, yet shall he live:
***26** And whosoever liveth and believeth in me shall*
never die. Believest thou this?

Martha was mourning the death of Lazarus. She was concerned that the Lord had tarried. She believed that if He were there, Lazarus would not have died. When Jesus mentioned His being the resurrection and the life, her mind was probably filled with a common Jewish belief that there would be a resurrection at the end of time.

We can tell from the context that Jesus' intention was to provide an immediate proof of His claim. Only one who is God could have commanded His dead friend to rise to life.

> *John 15:1*
> *1 I am the true vine, and my Father is the husbandman.*

Jesus reminds us that there is no other source from which to draw our strength for spiritual life. The Lord Jesus is the source, and the Father is the sovereign husbandman that keeps the vineyard. He knows just when to prune us and to apply the proper amount of nutrients to accomplish His goal of making us like His Son. He works in us and through us to complete His purpose (Hebrews 13:20, 21).

If the "I Am" passages do not point to Jesus being God, What do they mean?

We have provided a more complete list of the miracles Jesus performed in Appendix II. The following list is available as an example of His supernatural power to show that He is uniquely divine.

Jesus' miracles and signs prove His divinity.

(1) He turned the water into wine (John 2:1-11);

(2) He healed a son (John 4:46-54);

(3) He made a man whole (John 5:1-16);

(4) He fed a multitude (John 6:1-14);

(5) He stilled a storm (Mark 4:35-41);

(6) He gave sight to the blind (John 9:1-38); and

(7) He raised the dead (John 11:35-46).

All the above show that our Lord exercised authority over time, distance, disease, growth, gravitation, nature's power, and even death (John 20:30-31).

Because of Jesus' claims, the Jewish leadership sought to kill Him. They believed He was just an ordinary man. They thought His claim to be God was an act of presumption worthy of death. They probably thought that God could not possibly be a man. Is it possible they thought the Messiah was going to be a leader similar to Moses?

The majority chose to brand Jesus a heretic.

Some of the Jewish hierarchy actually believed Jesus was the Son of God and sought to learn from Him. Maybe others also knew but did not wish to submit to Him. Still, others were likely blinded by their prejudices and lust for religious power. Such sinful behavior is common in human organizations. Religious institutions are not immune to this plight.

Most Pharisees and Sadducees perceived Jesus to be a threat to their religious system. They did not believe Him to be whom He claimed and probably thought they were serving God in seeking Jesus' death much like Paul at the stoning of Stephen. Therefore, they accused Him of being a blasphemer and condemned Him to a Roman judgment and crucifixion.

They believed they were right. What a man believes may have nothing to do with facts or truth. A person may believe many things but that does not make his belief accurate. A man can believe that 2+2=5, but his belief does not make it true. What we believe only counts when what we believe is the "truth." Being sincere is not enough. Our sincerity must be based on conviction that has "truth" as its foundation.

In addition to the truths given above, we have the following facts that point to Jesus' deity: He is Creator of all things (John 1:3; Colossians 1:16); He is the Upholder of all things (Colossians 1:17); He is the Forgiver of sin (Mark 2:5-10).

Do you not agree that all this testimony to His deity is overwhelming?

Study Guide

1) List five characteristics that prove that Jesus is truly man.

2) What is the most likely reason the Jewish leaders rejected Jesus as God's Son and their Messiah?

3) What is the one thing that all men have done that Jesus did not do? Why did you give your answer?

4) List the I Am passages and indicate how each shows His deity.

5) Discuss why miracles and signs prove Jesus is God.

CHAPTER 4

WHAT JESUS TAUGHT: ABOUT THE HOLY SPIRIT

The Holy Spirit, as revealed in Scripture, is the third person of the **Trinity**. While the term **Trinity** never appears in Scripture, the concept is seen throughout both Testaments. Those who formulated the truths of Scripture into propositional concepts have adopted the term God-head. The term is used to describe a collective plurality in the midst of oneness. The concept of oneness in plurality is shown in Deuteronomy 6:4 where Moses wrote: "Hear, O Israel, the Lord our God is one Lord."

The verse is a declaration of Judaism's belief in one God. The belief separated them from their neighbors who believed in many gods. Notice Moses' unique use of the Hebrew language. The word "Lord" in Hebrew was Yahweh and considered too "holy" for the human tongue to utter. Therefore, they called Him Jehovah which is a vocalization of the tetragrammaton (YHWH). Another word for God in this verse is Elohim. Elohim is a plural noun. It may have reference to the Trinity, because it is the same noun used in God's description of His creating man as recorded in Genesis 1:26. In that verse He said, "And God said, Let us make man in our image, after our likeness . . ." Many Bible scholars believe the word **us** in the verse is a reference to the **Trinity**.

Therefore, when Jesus taught about the Holy Spirit He was discussing a third personality of the one true God. Understanding who the Holy Spirit is will aid us in knowing what the Lord Jesus taught about Him.

Jesus taught:
God Would Save Man
Through The Holy Spirit

John 3:5
5 Jesus answered, Verily, verily, I say unto thee,
Except a man be born of water and of the Spirit,
he cannot enter into the kingdom of God.

The verse above has been understood in various ways. It is beyond the scope of our search to analyze all possible meanings. However, several of the more popular views are as follows:

(1) Some teach that the word **water** is an act of baptism. If this was true, then for one to enter heaven, one would have to be baptized to experience spiritual conversion. Such an interpretation would be contrary for example to the heart of Ephesians 2:8, 9 where we are informed that salvation is of grace not of works or deeds or ceremonies.

(2) The use of water in this context is often believed to be a reference to John's (the Baptist) baptism as a sign of repentance. It is true that Nicodemus would have understood this in keeping with his Hebrew culture and the ceremonial cleansing through various washings with water. In keeping with this interpretation, after repentance, the Spirit of God would then introduce a new creation into the heart of the believer. He would thus be born of the **Spirit** or **born again**.

(3) A more likely possibility is that the **water** is symbolic of the Word of God. Therefore, as the Word is read and studied, it has a sanctifying effect on the soul. That interpretation would be in keeping with the words of Jesus when He said, "Sanctify them through thy truth: thy word is truth." (John 17:17) The Spirit then would through the Word, bring believers into unity with God by a spiritual process the Bible calls the new birth.

Regardless of the interpretation you choose to follow, one principle is clear from John's gospel chapter three: "Except a man be born of water and of the Spirit, he cannot enter into the kingdom of God." One cannot enter into God's presence without the Spirit bringing him into a new life that is likened unto a new birth.

Another verse that focuses on the Father using the Spirit to give souls the gift of eternal life is John 6:63.

John 6:63
It is the spirit that quickeneth; the flesh profiteth nothing: the words that I speak unto you, they are spirit, and they are life.

The word **spirit** is a reference to the Spirit of God. The word **quickeneth** refers to the action of the Spirit upon the soul when he exercises faith in Christ. Without the life-giving power of the Spirit, man in his flesh would be powerless to make himself acceptable to God. The Spirit reserves His life-giving power for those who trust Christ as their Savior from God's wrath against sin and unrepentant sinners. There are other references to the Spirit using God's Word to give life to repentant men by grace through faith (Ephesians 2:8,9). Here, it is clear that God alone can take a man who is **dead in sin** and give him **eternal life**. Such spiritual life is possible only through the work of the Holy Spirit.

Thus we see the Holy Spirit as the life-giving agent based on the will of the Father and the obedience of the Son. All partners of the Trinity are active in a person's salvation: The Father initiates salvation by making it available through His Son; the Son pays the redemption price for salvation through shedding His sinless blood; the Spirit applies salvation to the soul of the believer through the Word of God (Psalm 119:50, 93; Psalm 150; Hebrews 4:12).

Jesus Taught:
The Holy Spirit is a Gift

There has been much discussion about this point throughout the history of the Church. And most likely the difficulties are related to faulty assumptions about biblical statements. For example, we must consider the following verse in its natural environment. The verse is couched in the heart of a discussion about prayer. It is not a verse that may stand alone like John 3:16 or Deuteronomy 6:4. Most of God's Word must be considered in the context of its history, culture and grammatical construction. To ignore these realities is to run the risk of misusing or misinterpreting God's message.

In the context of Luke 11:13, the Lord is encouraging His disciples to be both bold and humble in making prayer requests. He goes on to use the analogy of a normal father providing his children their needs and assuring them that the heavenly Father would do no less. Then He says. . .

> *Luke 11:13*
> *13 If ye then, being evil, know how to give good gifts unto your children: how much more shall your heavenly Father give the Holy Spirit to them that ask him?*

At this point in the timeline of the Lord's life, He was primarily addressing His disciples as Jews. His whole earthly ministry was dedicated to a twofold mission: (1) to present Himself, in fulfillment of Scripture, to the Jews as their Messiah; (2) to glorify His father by resolutely setting His will to complete His Father's mission, doing this He became an acceptable sacrifice for all the sins of mankind. The Father had decreed before the foundations of the world that the Christ would be the sacrificial Lamb of God (Revelation 13:8).

After Jesus' resurrection He appeared to His disciples and He breathed on them and said, ". . .receive you the Holy Spirit (John 20:22)." The event took place between Christ's crucifixion and His ascension. The most likely reason He breathed on them was to provide them with an awareness of His presence. He had promised that the Father would send the Spirit. The apostles needed the presence of God's Spirit to face the many trials that would vex them while waiting for what God would do next. Therefore, when He appeared to them in their secluded safehouse He breathed on them and said: "Receive ye the Holy Ghost (John 20:22)."

The Church had not yet been introduced. The concept of an assembly of God's people apart from Judaism was still a mystery. That idea of a new covenant would not be made known until after Christ's ascension. It is true that the Lord had said to Peter ". . .on this rock I will build my church; . . . " (Mathew 16:18). No other instruction had been given about a unique assembly of God's people who would be known as the bride of Christ.

Therefore, Luke 11:13 may well have been a prophetical statement about the Holy Spirit's coming when He would baptize the church with His presence on the day of Pentecost. Remember, John the baptizer speaking of Jesus had said, ". . .the same is he which baptizeth with the Holy Ghost " (John 1:33).

We learn that the Father has sent His Spirit, upon promise of Jesus, to comfort, to guide and to teach His people under the new covenant. However, there is yet one other element to the promise. The Father not only wants believers to know Him, through the presence of the Spirit, but to live abundantly through His power.

John 7:37-39
37 In the last day, that great day of the feast, Jesus
stood and cried, saying, If any man thirst, let him come
unto me, and drink.
38 He that believeth on me, as the scripture hath said,
out of his belly shall flow rivers of living water.
39 (But this spake he of the Spirit, which they that be-
lieve on him should receive: for the Holy Ghost was
not yet given; because that Jesus was not yet
glorified.)

The baptism of the Spirit took place after Christ had as-cended into heaven. Most scholars believe that His return to the Father was the point of His glorification. At that time the Spirit was free to indwell the hearts of believers as the Lord had promised He would (John 14:26).

The Spirit is to be given to those who believe on Christ. Why? Because it is the only way they may live abundant lives to the glory of the Father. Christ uses the picture of a free flowing well to describe the abundant life. Just as the physical body must have physical water to survive, so must the spiritual life have spiritual water to live. There is no eternal life apart from the Spirit.

The abundant life is a life lived in the power of the Spirit. Paul paints a word picture of the abundant life when he describes the fruit of the Spirit in Galatians 5:22, 23. The fruit of the Spirit (love, joy, peace, longsuffering, etc) is seen in the life of one who, by God's grace, is living a life of victory over sin. They are those who refuse to be hin-dered by known sin. In the power of the Holy Spirit they reject the temptations to sin. They do this by calling on the Spirit to empower them. Christians cannot live an abundant life for Christ without the enabling power of the Holy Spirit's presence.

Jesus Taught :
The Spirit Indwells the Believer

John 14:17
17 Even the Spirit of truth; whom the world cannot receive, because it seeth him not, neither knoweth him: but ye know him; for he dwelleth with you, and shall be in you.

God's Spirit has dwelt among His people on only three occasions: (1) He indwelled the Tabernacle (Holy of Holies) in the wilderness in the midst of the tribe of Israel; (2) He indwelled the body of Jesus; (3) He presently indwells the souls of His people who make up the **Bride of Christ** and is called the Church. The coming of the Spirit into the hearts of believers would not take place until the birth of the Church on the day of Pentecost as recorded in Acts 2:1-4. From that point on the Holy Spirit baptizes every believer into Christ and seals him by His indwelling presence for the day of redemption (Ephesians 4:30).

Jesus Taught:
The Spirit Witnesses About Christ

There are a couple of passages that point to the Spirit's witness.

John 15:26
26 But when the Comforter is come, whom I will send unto you from the Father, even the Spirit of

truth, which proceedeth from the Father, he shall testify of me:

Notice the unique expression of how the Spirit is given. He is sent by Jesus, but He is from the Father. Once again we see the activity of the Trinity: the Son promises the Spirit as His gift; the Father is the source of the gift; the Holy Spirit is the gift. So we see clearly that God is active through His three personalities.

The verse reveals that the Spirit is given to fulfill two functions: (1) to comfort those whom He indwells; (2) to testify about Christ. One may well ask, to what does He testify? He affirms through the Spirit all that Christ claims in person and deed. For example, Jesus said, ". . .I am the way, the truth and the life (John 14:6)." The Spirit bears witness to all who have **ears** to hear that the words of Jesus are true and are affirmed by God the Father. The Spirit affirms the Bible to be the Word of God and the Spirit reaffirms every truth as the believer encounters the Word in Scripture and life. The Holy Spirit is God's faithful witness to the believer every moment of every day reaffirming the reality of Christ and His message.

From the following passage we are to discover even more about the Spirit's witness.

> *John 16:12-16*
> *12 I have yet many things to say unto you, but ye cannot bear them now.*
> *13 Howbeit when he, the Spirit of truth, is come, he will guide you into all truth: for he shall not speak of himself; but whatsoever he shall hear,*

*that shall he speak: and he will shew you things
to come.*
*14 He shall glorify me: for he shall receive of
mine, and shall shew it unto you.*
*15 All things that the Father hath are mine:
therefore said I, that he shall take of mine, and
shall shew it unto you.*
*16 A little while, and ye shall not see me: and
again, a little while, and ye shall see me, because I go to the Father.*

A full exposition of the above passage is beyond our purpose. But, I do want to call your attention to a key fact.
Jesus deliberately withheld certain information from His
disciples. Why? Perhaps, because they were not spiritually
ready to receive the things that were yet to come. He does
not give any clues as to what these things may have been.
But remember that these statements were made before the
writing of the New Testament. We now have the privilege
of looking through the prisms of the New Testament lens.
Therefore, we know that at the completion of the Bible we
have the complete mind of Christ.

He also informs us in verse thirteen that the Spirit will
bear witness to two things: (1) the truth of God; (2) the
things that are to come. He will teach us whatever we
need to know about the future. He witnesses in such a way
as to not draw attention to Himself but rather He focuses
attention on the Lord Jesus.

It is clear from the text that Christ only taught His disciples that which He received from the Father. In that same
manner the Spirit never glorifies Himself. The Spirit glorifies the Son by affirming the Son. The Son glorifies the

Father by giving to man only what He received from His Father.

In verse sixteen, the Holy Spirit reminds us again of Jesus' mission and what He accomplished on our behalf.

He told His disciples that in a little while they would not see Him. Why would they not see Him? Because He would have been crucified and buried in a tomb.

Then He told them that they would see Him in a little while. How could that be? Because, He knew He would be resurrected!

He then told them that He would go to His Father. This last bit of information is a reference to what we call **the ascension**. We believe that during the process of the resurrection and the ascension that Christ was received into a state of glorification with the Father.

All of the above was necessary for sinners like you and me to receive God's forgiveness for sin and be adopted into His family.

Jesus Taught: God will not Forgive Blasphemers of the Spirit

We will now consider one of the most troubling verses in the New Testament. It is found in Matthew 12:31.

Matthew 12:31
31 Wherefore I say unto you, All manner of sin and blasphemy shall be forgiven unto men: but the

blasphemy against the Holy Ghost shall not be forgiven unto men.

Many Christians have been concerned that they may have committed the unforgivable sin. One who believes in the Son of God as personal savior from the wrath of God need never be fearful of blaspheming the person of the Holy Spirit. First of all, the sin cannot be unwittingly committed. It is never done in ignorance.

What exactly is the sin? Members of the Jewish leadership had been threatened by the growing popularity of Jesus and the signs that proved that He was the Messiah. If He were the Messiah, they may have reasoned, what will happen to us when He becomes King? Of course these thoughts are conjecture. No one knows what was in the minds of the Pharisees and Sadducees. But one thing is clear. They had witnessed the power of the Spirit working through Christ. They saw Him raise the sick. They saw Him cast out demons. They calculatingly chose to ignore the obvious conclusion and leveled an outlandish lie that Christ did what He did by the power of Beelzebub (the prince of devils).

The sin described above is the unpardonable sin because those committing the sin chose to deliberately reject the Holy Spirit's witness that Christ was the Son of man and therefore the Jewish Messiah. Some hold that the sin could only be committed at that particular time in history. While there may be some truth in that position, I am more comfortable with the next statement.

Most conservative scholars have come to believe the following; the rejection of Christ by those religious leaders present in Matthew 12:31 presented a unique historical moment that cannot be reproduced in our own time. However, the essence of what they did can be done at any moment in any generation. What sin can be committed now that is ultimately unforgivable? It is the sin of rejecting Christ as your savior! For in rejecting Him, you reject the witness of the Holy Spirit who draws you to Christ. Therefore, you cannot be forgiven nor saved. For today, the rejection of Christ in effect becomes the unpardonable sin.

These are the key things that Jesus taught about God the Holy Spirit.

Study Guide

While our presentation has not been exhaustive in what our Lord taught about the Holy Spirit, perhaps it will whet your appetite for further independent study.

1. Based on John 6:33 how does the Holy Spirit save man?

2. Why does man need God's gift of the Holy Spirit?

3. When does the Holy Spirit take up His residence in the believer?

4. What two things about the Holy Spirit does John 15:26 reveal?

5. Why will God not forgive the blasphemers of the Holy Spirit?

CHAPTER 5

WHAT JESUS TAUGHT ABOUT THE DEVIL

Lucifer was an angel created to guard the throne of Jehovah God (Isaiah 14:12-14). His name means **light** or **the son of morning**. Sin was found in his heart, and God judged him. Because of his sin, he was cast down to earth with all the angels who followed him (Ezekiel 28:12-19). On earth he operates as the **prince of the power of the air** (Ephesians 2:2), **and god of this world** (2 Corinthians 4:4).

Lucifer is now known as Satan, meaning adversary. He is sometimes called the Devil and the dragon (Revelation 12:3). His name depicts what he does. He is an adversary—the enemy of Truth. The Devil opposes God and all who follow Him. He walks about seeking whom he may devour or destroy (1 Peter 5:8). He is also known as

Beelzebub the king or prince of demon spirits (Matthew 12:24).

Satan, as the god of this world, is manipulating the affairs of wicked men. He is filled with the desire to oppose and overcome God in every possible way. His strategies hinder the service of all Christians. Satan and his minions target faithful churches for persecution.

Jesus Taught:
Satan is the Source of Temptation

In the chapter dealing with what our Lord taught about temptation, we will share more extensively about how Satan works. For now we want to focus on the fact that the Devil is responsible for temptation.

> *Matthew 4:3-10*
> *3 And when the tempter came to him, he said, If thou be the Son of God, command that these stones be made bread.*
> *4 But he answered and said, It is written, Man shall not live by bread alone, but by every word that proceedeth out of the mouth of God.*
> *5 Then the devil taketh him up into the holy city, and setteth him on a pinnacle of the temple,*
> *6 And saith unto him, If thou be the Son of God, cast thyself down: for it is written, He shall give his angels charge concerning thee: and in their hands they shall bear thee up, lest at any time thou dash thy foot against a stone.*
> *7 Jesus said unto him, It is written again, Thou shalt not tempt the Lord thy God.*

8 Again, the devil taketh him up into an exceeding high mountain, and sheweth him all the kingdoms of the world, and the glory of them;
9 And saith unto him, All these things will I give thee, if thou wilt fall down and worship me.
10 Then saith Jesus unto him, Get thee hence, Satan: for it is written, Thou shalt worship the Lord thy God, and him only shalt thou serve.

The Holy Spirit directed Christ into the wilderness for the purpose of subjecting Him to Satan's temptation. We are not told in the text why the Lord was to be tempted. Perhaps from other Scriptural sources, we can conclude that there were at least two reasons: (1) to show that the Son of God was tempted in every way man can be tempted and still not sin (Hebrews 4:15) and (2) to show that where the **first Adam** failed, the **second Adam** or **last Adam** (Jesus) succeeds (1 Corinthians 15:20-23).

Ever since the first temptation of Adam and Eve in the garden, Satan has continued to use the stumbling block called temptation. The Devil was the first tempter and he will continue his iniquitous work until God calls it to an end.

Jesus Taught:
Satan is the Prince of Demons

Matthew 12:22-28
22 Then was brought unto him one possessed with a devil, blind, and dumb: and he healed him, insomuch that the blind and dumb both spake and saw.

23 And all the people were amazed, and said, Is not this the son of David?

24 But when the Pharisees heard it, they said, This fellow doth not cast out devils, but by Beelzebub the prince of the devils.

25 And Jesus knew their thoughts, and said unto them, Every kingdom divided against itself is brought to desolation; and every city or house divided against itself shall not stand:

26 And if Satan cast out Satan, he is divided against himself; how shall then his kingdom stand?

27 And if I by Beelzebub cast out devils, by whom do your children cast them out? therefore they shall be your judges.

28 But if I cast out devils by the Spirit of God, then the kingdom of God is come unto you.

The Lord Jesus identifies Satan as Beelzebub in Matthew 12:24. He was commonly believed to be the prince of demons. By using the term to explain the error of their argument, Jesus confirmed that Satan was the chief among demons.

We are not told in the Bible where demons come from. Most Bible teachers see them as another designation of the angels that followed Satan in his rebellion. One fact is certain, demons are spirit beings who are not to be confused with those **spirits in chains** as recorded in Jude 6. The spirits referred to in Jude are those that kept not their first estate and were immediately judged and placed in chains until the final judgment. (The **first estate** spirits are thought to be those sons of God spoken of in Genesis 6:4.)

At the judgment, they too will be consciously cast into the lake of fire.

Jesus Taught:
The Devil Fell from Heaven

In Luke, we have the Lord Jesus sending out the seventy to the towns and villages of Israel. After their successful campaign, the disciples returned rejoicing because of the power they had over the enemy.

Read what was written.

> *Luke 10:17-18*
> *17 And the seventy returned again with joy, saying, Lord, even the devils are subject unto us through thy name.*
> *18 And he said unto them, I beheld Satan as lightning fall from heaven.*

Contemplate the phrase, "I beheld Satan as lightening fall from heaven." When Christ made that statement He confirmed that He was present when the Father discovered sin in Lucifer's heart. He actually observed the proceedings as Satan was pronounced guilty of his rebellion. He saw Satan when he was cast down to the earth and banished from dwelling in heaven. Ever since that moment the Devil has been waging war on the purposes of God.

The fall Jesus speaks of ultimately includes judgment in the lake of fire prepared for Satan and his angels, sometimes called evil spirits (Matthew 25:41). We glean from this passage that Satan is a defeated foe who is presently dangerous as an adversary, but the victory is God's, and the destruction of the Devil's domination is guaranteed.

Jesus Taught:
The Devil Perverts Scripture

The Devil has quoted Scripture on numerous occasions. All his quotes are obviously not recorded in the Bible. However, when he does quote the Lord's Word, he either suggests that God does not mean what He says or God cannot be trusted. Let us consider an example.

> *Psalm 91:11-12*
> *11 For he shall give his angels charge over thee, to keep thee in all thy ways.*
> *12 They shall bear thee up in their hands, lest thou dash thy foot against a stone.*

The verses above were quoted by Satan in his temptation of Jesus (Mathew 4:1-11). The Devil had quoted it accurately, but facetiously. He was attempting to get the Lord to use His divine power in a way that would not please the Father. Jesus responded in obedience and quoted, "You shall not tempt the Lord your God" (Deuteronomy 6:16). By responding with this quote, He let Satan know that the Son of Man was committed to the Father's ministry.

Satan still perverts the use of Scripture in tempting believers to abandon our Father's will. For example, many naive Christians shy away from open criticism of evil activity because they fear violating a Scripture that the Devil misapplies. You have heard him quote it often. He often energies the spiritually ignorant to accuse faithful Christians by leading them to quote, ". . . Judge not that you be not judged . . ." (Luke 16:37). The verse is absolutely true—it is God's Word! However, the context in which it is often quoted is deceptive. The Christian is never to judge with the hope that the one judged would be harmed or hurt. The motive for applying Christian judgment should always be positive. Judgement's goal is to correct a life for redemption of either the person's soul or his life.

Jesus Taught: The Devil can Possess People

The Devil and his evil spirits sometimes called demons may possess people (Luke 8:26-33).

Luke 8:26-33
26 And they arrived at the country of the Gadarenes, which is over against Galilee.
27 And when he went forth to land, there met him out of the city a certain man, which had devils long time, and ware no clothes, neither abode in any house, but in the tombs.
28 When he saw Jesus, he cried out, and fell down before him, and with a loud voice said, What have I to do with thee, Jesus, thou Son of God most high? I beseech thee, torment me not.
29 (For he had commanded the unclean spirit to come out of the man. For oftentimes it had caught him: and he was kept bound with chains and in fetters; and he brake the bands, and was driven of the devil into the wilderness.)

81

30 And Jesus asked him, saying, What is thy name? And he said, Legion: because many devils were entered into him.
31 And they besought him that he would not command them to go out into the deep.
32 And there was there an herd of many swine feeding on the mountain: and they besought him that he would suffer them to enter into them. And he suffered them.
33 Then went the devils out of the man, and entered into the swine: and the herd ran violently down a steep place into the lake, and were choked.

In the case cited, some people deny the existence of supernatural elements. They seek to explain it away by suggesting that it is just a psychological issue such as a case of schizophrenia. They simply accuse Jesus of accommodating Himself to the superstitions of the times. There is a better answer!

Christ, being God incarnate in flesh, was beyond being a man of integrity. He never used the accommodation principle that is often employed in our society. Why? Because, it is deception. Jesus never deceived anyone; because that is the ploy of the Devil. It is best to interpret the passage at face value.

We learn from the above account that it is possible for agents of the Devil to take up residence within the personality of a person and possess that person's body for evil purposes. The man from Gadara, was thought to be out of his mind. However, he was actually possessed by many demons. These demons announced themselves when Jesus asked them for their name. They pronounced themselves to be "Legion" for they were many. Upon Jesus' command the demons left the man and went into a herd of swine. The demons drove the swine into the sea where they drowned.

We are not told how the man became possessed, but we are given some insight from the apostle Paul. He reminds us that we are servants of the one whom we obey (Romans 6:16). The Devil cannot take over a body without the person's permission. I do not mean to say that you need a conversation with Satan to accord him permission to control you. It is far more subtle than that. A person can give permission by yielding to temptation or by agreeing with the philosophy of the Devil.

It is recorded that Satan entered the heart of Judas Iscariot (Luke 23:3). Because he was energized by the Devil, he betrayed the Son of God. Judas bears the responsibility for this because he was basically agreeing with the enemy.

There is another illustration that claims our attention. The Lord had just informed His disciples of His impending death, burial, and resurrection. Peter could not bring himself to accept what Jesus said. Because he was in denial, he began to rebuke the Lord. Jesus turned to Peter and rebuked Satan! Why? Because, Satan was energizing Peter's thoughts (Luke 4:8). Peter was being controlled by his selfish desire not to see his Master die. After Jesus' rebuke, it appears that Peter immediately repented. A situation like Peter's reminds us that we have to be diligent. We must watch over our hearts, lest we fall prey to the enemy and find ourselves in league with him.[1]

---

1 For an extensive treatment of this subject see our book titled "Our Unseen Enemy."

Jesus Taught:
The Devil is Under Judgment

Matthew 25:41
41 Then shall he say also unto them on the left
hand, Depart from me, ye cursed, into everlasting
fire, prepared for the devil and his angels:

In Matthew 25:31-46, Jesus informs the disciples about a time of Gentile judgment. In His description, He alludes to the fact that Hell is a place of torment and that it was originally created for the Devil and his angels. In the Gospels, Jesus provides us references to man's final judgment. Regarding Satan's judgment, we find more detail in Jesus' revelation recorded by John. Let's look further!

Revelation 12:3-9
3 And there appeared another wonder in heaven;
and behold a great red dragon, having seven
heads and ten horns, and seven crowns upon his
heads.
4 And his tail drew the third part of the stars of
heaven, and did cast them to the earth: and the
dragon stood before the woman which was ready
to be delivered, for to devour her child as soon as
it was born.
5 And she brought forth a man child, who was to
rule all nations with a rod of iron: and her child
was caught up unto God, and to his throne.

6 And the woman fled into the wilderness, where she hath a place prepared of God, that they should feed her there a thousand two hundred and three-score days.

7 And there was war in heaven: Michael and his angels fought against the dragon; and the dragon fought and his angels,

8 And prevailed not; neither was their place found any more in heaven.

9 And the great dragon was cast out, that old serpent, called the Devil, and Satan, which deceiveth the whole world: he was cast out into the earth, and his angels were cast out with him.

In Revelation 12:3-9, we see a verbal description of the supernatural struggle being waged for the prize of God's creation. Satan and His angels have been cast down to the earth and is deceiving the whole world. We are not told when he was ejected from heaven.

There seems to be a reference to his ejection in Ezekiel 28:12-14. Though the Devil no longer dwells in heaven, he still must give an account of his activities until his final judgment (Job 1:6-12).

The mention of Michael's struggle with the Devil may have reference to the last three and one-half years of the "great tribulation."

Revelation 20: 1-3
3 And I saw an angel come down from heaven, having the key of the bottomless pit and a great chain in his hand.

*2 And he laid hold on the dragon, that old ser-
pent, which is the Devil, and Satan, and bound
him a thousand years,
3 And cast him into the bottomless pit, and shut
him up, and set a seal upon him, that he should
deceive the nations no more, till the thousand
years should be fulfilled: and after that he must be
loosed a little season.*

As we understand it, the timeline will flow as follows.
When the great tribulation concludes, certain things will
happen: 1) the Devil's persecution of Israel will be inter-
rupted, 2) Christ will come with angels to defeat the rebellious hordes of Satan, demons, and sinful men, and 3) the
Devil will be bound and cast into the pit for a thousand
years (Revelation 20:1-3).

The end is not yet! Look at the next reference.

*Revelation 20:7-10
7And when the thousand years are expired, Satan
shall be loosed out of his prison,
8 And shall go out to deceive the nations which
are in the four quarters of the earth, Gog and Ma-
gog, to gather them together to battle: the number
of whom is as the sand of the sea.
9 And they went up on the breadth of the earth,
and compassed the camp of the saints about, and
the beloved city: and fire came down from God out
of heaven, and devoured them.
10 And the devil that deceived them was cast into
the lake of fire and brimstone, where the beast and
the false prophet are, and shall be tormented day
and night for ever and ever.*

Christ and His saints will rule in righteousness for a thousand years. When the thousand years conclude, the Devil will be released from the pit for one final attempt at rebellion. The Devil will fail miserably! Satan with his angels, will be cast into the lake of fire and brimstone to be tormented forever. Thus, Jesus teaches us about the Devil's end.

For further study about what Jesus taught about the Devil—look up the following:

(1)　The Devil hinders the gospel

　　　(Mathew 13:19).

(2)　The Devil plants unbelievers among believers (Matthew 13:25).

(3)　The Devil's temptations can be resisted

　　　(Luke 22:46).

Study Guide

1. What is a tempter and what does tempting accomplish?

2. What kind of created being is the Devil?

3. What is a common way the Devil perverts Scripture?

4. How does the Devil hinder the gospel?

5. If the Devil is cast out of heaven, where is he now?

6. What will be the Devil's final judgment?

CHAPTER 6

WHAT JESUS TAUGHT ABOUT TEMPTATION

We will consider four key things our Lord Jesus taught about temptation. But first, let us differentiate between temptation and sin. Many do not know the difference. Some feel that even being tempted makes them sinful.

A vivid illustration was given by Billy Graham in one of his crusades. He reminded his audience that temptation was like a fly buzzing around looking for a place to land. Like the fly, you can shoo temptation away, but it becomes sin when you ignore it, and it builds its nest in your mind and you enjoy its presence.

If the illustration is a good analogy, then we can see that it is not a sin to be tempted. Temptation becomes sin when we agree with it in our hearts and engage it to enjoy its fruit. The engagement does not have to be actual to become sin. Mentally desiring the sin makes you guilty of the sin.

As we consider the following Scriptures, remember our goal is to 1) identify temptation, 2) reject it, 3) take God's side against the temptation and 4) turn from it.

Jesus Taught:
Satan is the Source of Evil

The Scripture informs us that sin originated in the heart of Satan (Ezekiel 28:12-15). It is also the Devil that tempts man, while using two faithful allies: (1) the **world** with its system of lust and greed, and (2) the **flesh** filled with its pride and selfishness. With these two allies, Satan has waged an effective war on man who is made in the image of God.

Why does Satan abhor man so? Could it not be that it is because we are made in God's image? A created being himself, the Devil is subject to the creator as are all created beings. One would reason, therefore, that he has become the adversary of God and everything God loves, because pride has filled his heart with the wicked desire to replace Jehovah as the Lord of all creation (Isaiah 14:12-15).

Knowing something of Satan, we can understand more why our Lord led his disciples to pray "deliver us from temptations of the evil one (paraphrase)." In the prayer that Jesus modeled for His disciples, He offered the following:

> *Matthew 6:13*
> *13 And lead us not into temptation, but deliver us from evil: For thine is the kingdom, and the power, and the glory, for ever. Amen.*

The phrase "...lead us not into temptation" may give the false impression that God leads us into temptation. But, James reminds us that God tempts no one (James 1:13). Therefore, it most likely would mean—lead us not into the trials of hardship or persecution from the evil one. The Greek scholar, Marvin R. Vincent, says of this phrase—"It means trial of any kind, without reference to its moral quality." Therefore, the believer may pray for deliverance from any trial that is intended to cause him to fail as a Christian. However, it should be understood that God will allow such persecutions and adversities when it is His will that you are strengthened through the trial.

The Lord also told His disciples to pray for deliverance. Why? Because, the Evil One and his minions are allowed to tempt and try us. Why? Because it is the enemy's purpose to entrap us as prey. While the Lord allows these trials (by temptation) from the Devil, God Himself tempts no one. Because of this, some say that Satan is God's errand boy sent to accomplish the ultimate purpose of God. That conclusion causes some uneasiness in us because it makes it sound that God is promoting temptation. That is not true! The thought may contain an element of truth when you bring God's sovereignty into the equation.

God is sovereign! Therefore, He reigns over all His created beings (including Satan), man, and all living creatures. He also reigns over the galaxies and universes known and unknown. Such authority is difficult for us to comprehend or even imagine, but it is what Scripture teaches (Colossians 1:16, 17).

While the Father created Lucifer—who became Satan the adversary—He did not create sin or evil. He created the possibility for evil for purposes only known to Him. What we do know is that evil (as iniquity) was found in the heart of Satan (Ezekiel 28:15). We ascertain from the Book of Job that the Devil has to give an account of himself to God (Job 1:6-12). Satan is then allowed to use his ploys in tempting man to do evil. As in the case with Job, Satan has to receive permission from God before he can even approach a Christian. God's goal in allowing such activity is that believers may have their character and faith strengthened through the trial. God never promised to deliver Christians from the difficulties that are common (in a fallen world) to all men. What He promised is that He will walk with us through the trials and He will not allow difficulties too heavy for us to bear (1 Corinthians 10:13).

Why? What is the purpose of temptation? From Satan's viewpoint, it is to enslave the souls of men for his service and to deny them the privilege of knowing and serving Jehovah. Remember man becomes the servant of the one to whom he yields himself. From God's viewpoint, it may be to reveal Himself to man or woo him into His service. Since God knows all things, temptation would not serve the purpose of enlightening Him. God knows us and He knows what we will do in any given situation.

If He knows everything, then why do we need temptation in our life? There are at least two reasons why God allows Christians to go through trials: (1) that His people may bear testimony to unbelievers about how people of grace handle life's trials and (2) that we may know ourselves and understand even more about how dependent we are on God and His sustaining mercy. In each of the above purposes—God receives glory.

In Matthew 6:13, we encountered the dilemma of evil and determined that Satan was its source. We also learned that God allows Christians to face various temptations for specific purposes.

Now in Matthew 4:1, 2 we see that God's own Son was not exempt from the trials of life.

> *Matthew 4.1, 2*
> *1 Then was Jesus led up of the Spirit into the wilderness to be tempted of the devil.*
> *2 And when he had fasted forty days and forty nights, he was afterward an hungred. (Mark 1.13; Luke 4.2)*

Here, we see our Lord Jesus as the Son of Man facing the insidious and deceptive ploys of Satan. God does not reveal why Christ was led into the wilderness to be tested.

Though not stated, we can glean at least four possible reasons why the Holy Spirit led the Lord into the wilderness: (1) for Him to experience in His flesh all the types of temptation to which man is subjected; (2) to show that the Word of God is more than sufficient to meet any trial that Satan can place before believers; (3) to reveal the superior power of the Spirit over the ploys generated by Satan; (4) to show that Jesus' experience in the wilderness served as a foretaste of God's ultimate victory over the Devil and his fallen angels.

Jesus Taught:
Temptation Comes to Three
of Life's Arenas

When Jesus faced the Devil in the wilderness, He was subjected to an attack in three areas of life. These areas are common to all men. Every believer faces temptation in these same areas: body, soul and spirit. We may refer to these as "Arenas of Conflict."

> *Matthew 4:3*
> *3 And when the tempter came to him, he said, If thou be the Son of God, command that these stones be made bread.*

After the Lord had fasted forty days and nights he was hungry. His body craved food. He needed nourishment to sustain His life. Now in His physical weakness, the Devil insidiously suggests that Jesus turn a rock into bread. (Satan brought doubt into the picture by using the phrase ". . .if thou be the son of God.") Jesus could have done what was suggested and by the miracle prove who He was. However, His doing so would have been a misuse of the Father's power. Why? Because, as the Son of Man, His eating was to have been practiced as a normal man. A natural man with natural powers would have been powerless to provide for himself in a miraculous manner. Therefore, performing a miracle to meet His own needs would have been an illegitimate use of His power at that particular time.

Christians are temples of the Holy Spirit. We do not have the right to fulfill our physical appetites in a manner that does not please our Father. When our bodily appetites become intense the Devil will tempt us to fulfill our hunger or desire in a way that would bring dishonor to God. For example, Christians are allowed to eat anything provided they can offer thanksgiving to God. However, we are not allowed to be glutinous. We should **not live to eat** but rather **eat to live**. Therefore eating a banana split after every meal would not bring glory to God. Does God care about what I eat? You bet He does!

Satan not only attacked the physical body of Jesus but His soul as well.

> *Matthew 4:5, 6*
> *5 Then the devil taketh him up into the holy city,*
> *and setteth him on a pinnacle of the temple,*
> *6 And saith unto him, If thou be the Son of God,*
> *cast thyself down: for it is written, He shall give*
> *his angels charge concerning thee: and in their*
> *hands they shall bear thee up, lest at any time thou*
> *dash thy foot against a stone.*

The Devil tempted Jesus to presume upon His position as the Son of God. Jesus had the right to every aspect of heavenly and earthly glory that His deity afforded Him. However, He was not free to use His power for Himself, but for the witness that He was God's Son and Israel's Messiah. His mission was to die on the cross of Calvary. His selfless death was to be for the sins of the world.

Through His sacrifice sin and death would be destroyed. Satan and his fallen angels would be defeated, and the entirety of creation could be restored to the glory of the Father—a world without sin. If the Devil could tempt Jesus to focus on Himself at the expense of His mission, then Satan would have gained the victory. Jesus refused to fall for the Devil's strategy.

Satan's ploys have not changed! He still seeks to divert Christians from their mission. What is the Christian's mission? There are at least four aspects of the mission: (1) worship God; (2) live faithful lives; (3) witness to the faithfulness of God; and (4) make disciples of those who believe the witness. When you yield to temptation, you will invariably violate your mission.

Satan also attacked Christ in His Spirit.

> *Matthew 4:8, 9*
> *8 Again, the devil taketh him up into an exceeding high mountain, and sheweth him all the kingdoms of the world, and the glory of them;*
> *9 And saith unto him, All these things will I give thee, if thou wilt fall down and worship me.*

There is a sense in which the temptation to worship someone or something other than Jehovah is to commit the sin of idolatry. For a Christian to do so amounts to spiritual adultery. If the Devil could get Jesus to worship him, the mission would have failed and the glory of God would have been tarnished.

Note that Jesus did not dispute Satan's claim. He knew the Devil had the authority to give Him all the world's glory should He worship him. Why? Because, Satan's authority rested in the fact that he is the **prince of the power of the air** (Ephesians 2:2) and the **ruler of this world** (John 12:31). At some point in time God appointed Lucifer as the ruler of the world. As **ruler** and **prince** of **evil** and of the **world system**, he has filled the world with greed, hate, and self-centeredness. It was from this position that Satan poised himself to launch his attack on Christ and His disciples and to corrupt all God loved.

Christ refused Satan's temptation because He was at one with His Father, and He refused to allow His loyalty to be divided. The Devil's strategy attacked the very core of Jesus' being and personality. It was an attack on His Spirit. Yielding to this temptation would terminate Christ's mission.

When we as believers are tempted to worship another god, person, or thing, our life purpose is threatened. If we succumb, we fall prey to Satan's lies and enter the service of sin.

Jesus not only taught us that Satan would attack us in every arena of life, but He also shared how to ward off those temptations. Earlier, we cited Paul's promise that God would not allow us to be tempted beyond our capacity to resist (1 Corinthians 10:13). Therefore, in the midst of temptations, we know that God will grant us His grace when we are obedient.

Jesus Taught:
Temptation is Defeated by the Word

Jesus resisted each temptation by applying a quotation from the Word of God. Note the following.

> *Matthew 4:4*
> *4 But he answered and said, It is written, Man*
> *shall not live by bread alone, but by every word*
> *that proceedeth out of the mouth of God.*

When Jesus was tempted to turn the stone into bread, He quoted from Deuteronomy. All His defense in the Matthew passage came from the same book. In this first case, it appears He used Deuteronomy 8:3.

Later in His ministry Jesus declared to His disciples: "My meat is to do the will of him that sent me, and to finish his work" (John 4:34). It becomes clear that as the Lord spiritually fed on the will of His Father, so must we. Do not allow yourself to be deterred by the sublime affections of this world. Nothing will really satisfy the Christian except the spiritual food from the Father. As Jesus fed on His Father's Word, so must our sustenance be "every Word that proceeds from the mouth of God."

> *Matthew 4:7*
> *7 Jesus said unto him, It is written again, Thou*
> *shalt not tempt the Lord thy God.*

The second temptation is directed to the **soul**. Jesus deflects Satan's fiery temptation by declaring Himself to be God. Being God, He is Lucifer's creator! Jesus reminds the adversary that as God He is the Devil's God. No created being can rise above his creator. Satan, as brilliant as he is, is playing the fool when he tries to test the Lord.

Jesus quotes again from God's Word (Deuteronomy 6:16). It is in the context of Israel's wilderness journey where at Massah, the grumbling Israelites put the Lord to the test.

They had angrily demanded that Moses provide them water where there was none. God in His faithfulness provided the needed water by having Moses speak to the rock (Exodus 17:3-6; Numbers 20:8-11). Moses, in his anger, struck the rock twice. His display of anger was an affront to God. Moses had exercised his authority in an illegitimate manner. Unlike Moses, Jesus refused to fall for Satan's ploy and rejected the temptation. Our Lord honored His position as God's Son.

As we have written before, Jesus was both God and man. As Son He was just as fully God as His father. But as man, His role was one of submission. He came to do the will of His Father. If He had flung Himself from atop the temple, He would have been acting outside the Father's will! Jesus refused to do it. He refused to tempt the Lord God His Father. He was victorious over the attack on His soul.

> *Matthew 4:10, 11*
> *10 Then saith Jesus unto him, Get thee hence, Satan: for it is written, Thou shalt worship the Lord thy God, and him only shalt thou serve.*
> *11 Then the devil leaveth him, and, behold, angels came and ministered unto him.*

The third of the temptations came to Jesus as a threat to the very core of His **Spirit**. He was invited to bow down and worship Satan. Jesus' simple response was to quote the Word of God. He refused to abandon His allegiance to His Father. In this verse Christ was citing and paraphrasing Deuteronomy 6:13, 14.

It has not been revealed what might have gone through the mind of our Lord during and after those days of fasting.

But from experience, we know that with just one day of denying our physical needs brings an accompanying weakness, weariness, and even emotional stress.

During these times of physical, spiritual, and emotional attack Satan will often suggest that God is nothing more than the creation of man's own imagination. The Devil will say things like: It is all just a fairy tale and there is nothing to life; when you are dead—you are dead! Awful things have come to mind. The Devil would suggest: there is no accountability! Go ahead, he would say, fulfill the desires of your flesh! Such reasoned thoughts would tempt one to leave his testimony and faith. Then, God in His faithfulness gently reminds the believing soul that, "Satan is a liar and the father of lies" and "Jesus is the Way, the Truth, and the Life (John 14:6)." God is the source and giver of **life**, and **eternal life** comes through Christ alone.

God's truth will always repel the fiery darts of Satan's temptations. But, if we do not know the "truth" it is of no effect. The Word of God will do no good as long as it is left on the coffee table, mantle, or bedside stand. It is food for the soul and must be digested daily by a believing heart. Only then, will its power be realized! Knowing your Father can only come by spending time with Him. He shares His truth with those who believe and obey. However, you will never know what pleases the Father if you do not spend time with Him in His Word.

Jesus Taught :
Temptation may be Resisted by Watching and Praying

Near the end of His earthly ministry, Jesus said:

> *Matthew 26:41*
> *41 Watch and pray, that ye enter not into tempta-*
> *tion: the spirit indeed is willing, but the flesh is*
> *weak. (Luke 22:40)*

We have a clear statement of what we should do to mini-mize attacks from the Devil and his demons. The Lord left us with two pieces of information. Both are vital to our success as Christians. They are: (1) the **spirit** of the be-liever is willing, but, (2) the believer's **flesh** is weak.

The believer is willing in spirit to go and do anything he knows the Father wills. The question is: What is His will? There is really no secret as to the Father's will for His children. It is clearly laid out in His Word. He desires that we: (1) follow the leading of the Holy Spirit (2) commune with Him daily through the Word and prayer (3) witness to His saving grace through Christ, and (4) obey Him when you know His will.

The thing that hinders us from doing His will is the weak-ness of our flesh. Why is our flesh weak? The key to an-swering that question is to understand the term **flesh**. The flesh is not biological matter such as skin, sinew, and bones. We are not referencing bodily flesh and blood. The **flesh** used in this context is the sin prone nature that re-sides in all mankind since the sin of Adam and Eve. The **flesh** or **sin nature** offers a natural resistance to what God Spirit is leading the Christian to do. I believe it was for this reason that Jesus said: "The flesh is weak."

The Christian has the Spirit of God indwelling him. There-fore, the Spirit in you is always at one with the will of the

Father. It was for this reason Jesus said: "The spirit is willing." The simple key to following God is found in Daniel Towner's hymn *Trust and Obey*: "trust and obey there is no other way to be happy in Jesus but to trust and obey."

The Lord tells us in the verse to **watch** and **pray**.

When we—as believers—are tempted to sin, and choose to yield, we may enjoy the fruit of sin momentarily. Soon after, when the sin has yielded its pleasure, you will begin to sense the grieving presence of the Holy Spirit. His convicting power will rest heavily upon your heart until you repent, confess, and ask for forgiveness (1 John 1:8-10).

Study Questions

Remember, do not confuse temptation with sin! Do not deceive yourself into thinking that sin is only committed when you act upon it. We are even guilty of sin when we agree with the temptation and desire to have its fruit. Regardless of the reason for not acting on the desire, the heart still desires it. Thus it is sin! That is why Jesus referred to the fact that one is guilty of adultery when he agrees with the desire in his heart. Therefore, sin is a matter of the heart.

1. What is the source of temptation?

2. What are the arenas of temptations as discussed in this chapter?

3. What did Jesus do to resist and reject temptations?

4. What are the two elements that will minimize the effects of temptations?

CHAPTER 7

WHAT JESUS TAUGHT ABOUT ETERNAL LIFE

Before we can take up Jesus' teaching on eternal life, we first must understand what we need to be saved from and why. (See *Chapter One* for it provides a background for understanding why mankind needs God's salvation.)

Every person existing after Adam and Eve has inherited a sin nature. That means we have an inbred tendency to be drawn to self-centeredness, selfishness, and self-glory. It is natural for us to seek fulfillment of our own desires without concern for the will of God. In this state, we are alienated from God. Unless something is done to restore us and to provide a way to escape His judgment, all mankind is lost. All humanity is like a mighty river rushing toward the fires of eternal judgment—a judgment God prepared for Satan and his fallen angels (Matthew 25:41).

In the era of Christ's ministry, many believed personal salvation is obtained in one of the following means: (1) by being born into a tribe that came from the loins of Abraham; or (2) by obeying the Ten Commandments; and (3) some believed that salvation came by perfectly observing the various rituals and sacrificial ceremonies of Judaism.

Jesus taught about eternal life against a backdrop of ignorance and false presuppositions.

Jesus Taught: Man Desires Assurance of Eternal Life

We know eternal life is a state of being that men desire. For example, we have at least two occasions recorded in the Gospels where men asked Jesus the question: What must I do to inherit eternal life? People search for eternal life for various reasons. It is impossible for one person to know the motive of another's heart. The one possible exception is one knowing his own heart. However, we often reveal our heart's motives by our actions.

There are two events that will yield some light on our study: the **Rich Young Ruler** (Matthew 19:16-22) and the **Lawyer** (Luke 10:25). We will first consider the Matthew 19 passage and its context.

> *Matthew 19:16-22*
> *16 And, behold, one came and said unto him,*
> *Good Master, what good thing shall I do, that I*
> *may have eternal life?*

17 And he said unto him, Why callest thou me good? there is none good but one, that is, God: but if thou wilt enter into life, keep the commandments.

18 He saith unto him, Which? Jesus said, Thou shalt do no murder, Thou shalt not commit adultery, Thou shalt not steal, Thou shalt not bear false witness,

19 Honour thy father and thy mother: and, Thou shalt love thy neighbour as thyself.

20 The young man saith unto him, All these things have I kept from my youth up: what lack I yet?

21 Jesus said unto him, If thou wilt be perfect, go and sell that thou hast, and give to the poor, and thou shalt have treasure in heaven: and come and follow me.

22 But when the young man heard that saying, he went away sorrowful: for he had great possessions.

Jesus left the region of Galilee and came into the district of Judea. Here, he was approached by Pharisees who engaged Him about marriage and divorce. It was after these interviews with the Pharisees and the children that a young man approached Him.

The man is called the young ruler. He approached Jesus addressing Him as Good Master. In using the title Good Master he was probably doing nothing more than using a respectful greeting. He may have witnessed the encounter with the Pharisees and with the children and might have been impressed in his heart that this was not an ordinary teacher. He may have even earlier heard about what Jesus was doing and teaching. He recognized Jesus was righteous and a teacher come from God. He probably thought that since Jesus had this **life**, He could tell him how he could be assured of having it by giving him the **formula**.

Jesus responded by saying: Why do you call me good? Then, He said: There are none good but God. The Lord knew that young man had not recognized Him. He did not realize that Jesus was the incarnate Son of God. Then, Jesus told him to keep the commandments if he wanted to enter "life." (The only way a person can enter heaven or eternal life, is to perfectly keep the moral code of God as expressed in **the commandments**.) God is not a cruel task master. He does not set a man up to fail. The law was given that we may understand the heart of God's holy character and that we may know ourselves. Our inability to keep it should cause us to reach out to God for mercy.

Jesus' charge keep the commandments was an impossible task for this young ruler or anyone. But, he was ignorant of that fact. In his present state, he was deceived. He believed that he had kept the commandments from his childhood. But, he would ask for the Lord to clarify. Therefore, he asked: Which commandments?

The Lord Jesus then listed six of the ten commandments that the Father had given Moses on Mt. Sinai. He quickly responded: *All these things have I kept from my youth up; what lack I yet?* But, the young ruler's heart had deceived him. He had believed that by using the Rabbi's standard, he had already kept the Law of God. He brashly said so!

The Lord Jesus did not rebuke him. He did not accuse him of lying. He simply said, *If thou wilt be perfect, go and sell all that thou hast, and give to the poor, and thou shalt have treasure in heaven: and come and follow me.*

His inquiry may suggest that he believed that some of the commandments were of greater value than others or that he only had to give an account for the ones Jesus would list. Where would he get such an understanding? It appears that over time, various Rabbis had re-interpreted the laws so that man could justify themselves before God. He took this position because, according to rabbinic instruction, he likely believed himself to have outwardly kept the commandments.

When Jesus gave the sermon on the mount, He made it clear that keeping His law was a matter of the heart. For example: He taught that unjustified anger toward someone was murder and lusting after someone was adultery. Such teaching shows us that God looks at the motive of the heart, because the heart drives the action of the hand and because all men are sinners and in need of salvation (Mathew 5:21-30).

Notice the elements of the Lord's instruction: 1) sell what you have, 2) give it to the poor, and 3) come follow Me. When the rich young ruler understood the cost of being a disciple of Jesus, he sorrowed and went away because he had many possessions. It appears that he could now see that his primary hindrance to following Christ was covetousness. The gospel of Jesus Christ is simple and free for all who will trust Christ, but trusting Him will cost you your life. In following Him we give over our lives to Him. We lose all our rights because they are transferred to Him. We cannot serve two masters (Mathew 6:24). We will either serve Christ or self. When we serve self we serve the Devil.

It is interesting that theses six Commandments were the ones that govern human relationships. These may be the most difficult for us to obey because they require you to look out for the needs of others while possibly subjecting yourself to neglect. That is what Jesus did—He gave Himself away.

Consider the lawyer who tested Jesus by asking about eternal life. What could have been his motivation for asking about eternal life?

Luke 10:25-29
25 And, behold, a certain lawyer stood up, and tempted him, saying, Master, what shall I do to inherit eternal life?
26 He said unto him, What is written in the law? how readest thou?
27 And he answering said, Thou shalt love the Lord thy God with all thy heart, and with all thy soul, and with all thy strength, and with all thy mind; and thy neighbour as thyself.
28 And he said unto him, Thou hast answered right: this do, and thou shalt live.
29 But he, willing to justify himself, said unto Jesus, And who is my neighbour?

Note that the lawyer—who was a scribe and considered an expert in the Law—was doing what lawyers do when he tempted Jesus with his question. His choice of words reveals that his question was not a search for truth but an attempt to ensnare Jesus in a contradiction. It appears that his motive was to discredit the Lord through a debate over the Law.

When he used the term Master it was probably used in a respectful but caustic manner. If we had been asked in the twenty-first century about how to find eternal life, our answer would have been different from that of our Lord's. Why? It would be different because of the historical and cultural context.

Our Lord was dealing with His own people who had misconceptions about how to please God. These erroneous understandings were based on faulty views of the Law and the sacrificial system. Jesus did not come to destroy but to fulfill the Law. Jesus "was" the fulfillment of the Law. But, His mission had not yet been completed. During His earthly life, Jesus chose to reveal Himself by example and precept. The Jews had both the Old Testament Scripture and His teaching (affirmed by His miracles) to identify Him as their Messiah. They stubbornly refused!

Therefore, in keeping with His purpose, Jesus answered the lawyer's question by asking: What is written in the law? What is your reading of it? The lawyer responded by quoting Deuteronomy 6:5 and Jesus commended him by saying: *You have answered rightly; this do and you will live.*

Jesus' answer is consistent with what the epistles of The New Testament teach us. In the epistles—Romans through Jude—we are taught how to know God and how to live for Him. We are taught that eternal life is a gift from God as a result of our having placed our faith in His testimony. He is justified, therefore, in granting us grace because we came to Him in faith. Because of faith placed in Christ the Holy Spirit takes up residence within us and begins to produce the fruit of the Spirit through us.

What Jesus said to the rich young ruler and the lawyer was not out of step with what the apostles taught in The New Testament Scriptures. Here is why! In each case, the instructions were the same—obey the commandments of God. No one can keep the Law of God without the Spirit and love of God motivating him. Those who had heard Jesus' instruction should have been smitten by guilt. Why? Because they would have realized themselves to be Law breakers and in need of God's mercy. God has always forgiven sin and granted mercy because of faith in His Word.

There are possibly three motives for desiring eternal life: 1) you want to love God and enjoy Him forever, 2) you intuitively know there is life beyond the grave and you want to be ready, and 3) you want to be assured that God will receive you as His own when you have to give an accounting. It appears that the lawyer had none of these motives.

Jesus Taught: Eternal Life has a Heavenly Source

There are at least two references that claim our attention. We begin by looking to John 5:23, 24.

> *John 5:23, 24*
> *23 That all men should honour the Son, even as they honour the Father. He that honoureth not the Son honoureth not the Father which hath sent him. 24 Verily, verily, I say unto you, He that heareth my word, and believeth on him that sent me, hath everlasting life, and shall not come into condemnation; but is passed from death unto life.*

It is interesting that the Gospel of John is the only one of the Gospels that uses such direct language regarding the personal relational aspects of salvation. The Scriptures declare throughout both testaments that salvation has only one source—God the Father. The Father sanctioned salvation for us; the Son procured salvation for us by His sacrificial death and resurrection; and the Spirit sealed salvation for all who trust in Christ.

In the passage above John writes about the relational closeness of the Father and the Son in his reference to honor. He said you could not honor one without honoring the other. Jesus said in verse twenty-four: *". . . I say unto you, He that hears my word, and believes on him that sent me, has everlasting life, . . ."* Jesus makes it clear that He is sharing the Father's message of how to know you have eternal life. He reveals to us that we must believe on the Father who sent Jesus. Why? Belief in God's message is necessary, because the Father is offering salvation only to those who receive His Word. His Word is Jesus (John 1:1).

Now let us closely look at John 17:3.

> *John 17:3*
> *And this is life eternal, that they might know thee the only true God, and Jesus Christ, whom thou hast sent.*

The verse is part of Jesus' personal prayer. Some call it His High Priestly Prayer. Why? Because in this prayer, Jesus takes the position of a priest interceding for His people and their needs. In this third verse He expresses His purpose in praying and also defines eternal life. Life eternal is knowing the one true God. Remember, if you know the Father, you will know the Son. The Father reveals the Son, and the Son reveals the Father. You cannot know one without knowing the other. The **key** to understanding is in unlocking the word **know**.

The Greek word for **know** is a verb, and it has to do with both perception and experience. It is the act of experiencing the reality of something or someone through information. In our case, it is experiencing the reality of God through His Word by His Spirit to our spirit (Romans 8:16). Therefore, the source of eternal life is Almighty God! Life through salvation is from the Father, bought by the Son, and administered by His Spirit. Jesus Taught:

Eternal Life is a Gift

> *John 3:16*
> *For God so loved the world, that he gave his only*
> *begotten Son, that whosoever believeth in him*
> *should not perish, but have everlasting life.*

It is clear from the verb gave that God has provided the gift of eternal life. As we expand the truths in the verse, the believer is blessed. Some years ago, on my way back from a meeting in another city, I began to dissect the meaning of John 3:16. The Lord began to unfold the verse to me as I meditated upon its content. In the following chart you will find the result of my contemplation. I have listed the key words and phrases that make up the verse and the truths taught by each one.

GOD'S SALVATION FOR MAN - JOHN 3:16

WORD or PHRASE	FOCUS or SUBJECT	OBSERVATION or APPLICATION
"For God"	GOD	the one who initiates salvation
"so loved"	LOVE	the motive for salvation
"the world"	WORLD	the object of His salvation
"that He gave"	GAVE	the act of salvation (the act of His giving us grace)
"His only begotten"	SON	the cost of salvation
"that whosoever"	WHOSOEVER	the inclusiveness of salvation
"believeth"	BELIEVE	the response of saving faith
"in Him"	CHRIST	the object of saving faith
"should not perish"	PERISH	the escape of saving faith (thru faith we escape wrath)
"but have"	HAVE	the possession of saving faith
"everlasting life."	LIFE	the result of saving faith

Over the years, my thinking about these truths has blessed me. The content of this simple verse is amazingly profound.

John 10:15 speaks of Eternal Life as a gift, and two things are apparent: (1) Not only has the Father loved the world —His creation and all in it—and given His Son for it (2) He has also redeemed His creation in that process. What process? The process called salvation. By sending His Son to die in payment for sin, He has redeemed all who in faith will come to Him. Therefore, only those who will not come will suffer the curse of spiritual death—eternal separation from God in the lake of fire.

> *John 10:15*
> *15 As the Father knoweth me, even so know I the Father: and I lay down my life for the sheep.*

Jesus emphasizes again His unique knowledge of the Father. The **knowing** He speaks of is a communion of His Spirit with the Father's Spirit. Jesus promises that the characteristic of knowing His Father is given to those who receive Him (Jesus).

Jesus gave the gift of His life so that all who believe or trust in Him can know the Father and thereby receive the gift of Life. God is so gracious to repeat the salvation message over and over. He laid down His life to save sinners like you and me from an eternal separation from the Father and a destiny in Hell.

Jesus Taught:
Eternal Life has an Element of Works

Let me first give a disclaimer; eternal life is not given because of one's work. However, listen to what Jesus says:

> *John 5:28, 29*
> *28 Marvel not at this: for the hour is coming, in the which all that are in the graves shall hear his voice,*

29 And shall come forth; they that have done good, unto the resurrection of life; and they that have done evil, unto the resurrection of damnation.

Notice the word **done**. It is a reference to physical actions taken by people who have been resurrected. What has been done in our life is made up of our life's work. Those, who have done good, will receive the reward of the blissful presence of God forever—the result of possessing eternal life. You are probably asking: Why are works mentioned? Because, works are the fruit of your life.

When you trusted Christ to save you, you were cleansed and forgiven of your sins. Christ's righteousness was credited to you. You were then spiritually baptized into the person of Christ and indwelled by the Holy Spirit. From that point on you have been enabled by the Spirit to serve Christ. How? The Spirit is working in you the desires of the Father. The works you experience as a believer, are the works that God commends on the day of resurrection. You will be rewarded for works but not saved by works.

But, you ask: What happens if I sin and do not obey Him?

He has made provision for that!

When a Christian sins, the Holy Spirit immediately convicts him. If he does not repent, the Holy Spirit is grieved and withdraws His fellowship. His assurance and fellowship will not be restored until he (1) repents—judges his sin and takes a stand with God against his own sins (2) confesses the sin or sins and (3) claims His forgiveness on the basis of 1 John 1:8-10.

Christian! Be warned! Do not presume to sin willfully. Do not think that you can presumably exercise the **First John** provision on the spur of the moment. One must first offer genuine repentance before forgiveness can begin. We cannot **con** God! He knows the heart. Repentance must be experienced before we can approach our Father for forgiveness. Many have sought to repent with tears and could not find it (Hebrews 12:17). Repentance begins by our judging our own sins before seeking His forgiveness.

From the believer's viewpoint, any known unconfessed sin will be dealt with at the judgment seat of Christ as described in 1Corinthians 3:11-17. If a believer finds himself in such a state, the Scripture indicates he will be saved as by fire. Remember, sin must be judged and forgiven—it cannot be excused!

> *John 12:25, 26*
> *25 He that loveth his life shall lose it; and he that hateth his life in this world shall keep it unto life eternal.*
> *26 If any man serve me, let him follow me; and where I am, there shall also my servant be: if any man serve me, him will my Father honour.*

The Christian life is a life marked by self-denial. As it was with the Savior, it must also be the mark of His disciples. We will enlarge upon this in a later chapter. Nothing could be clearer than our Lord's declaration above in verse twenty-six. Followers of Christ will serve Christ and will then be honored by the Father.

Good works from these passages speak of our service prompted by the Spirit. It is Christ working in us, through the Spirit that gives evidence that we are possessors of God's eternal life. This is not the idea that eternal life is earned by some deed or merit, but rather that our lives have a mark of eternity upon them and therefore spontaneously produce acts of godliness. **The Bible knows nothing of a life touched by Jesus and given the gift of eternal life that serves itself.**

Jesus Taught:
Eternal Life is a Present Reality

It has occurred to me that the greatest need in the Church of Jesus Christ is the need for a conscious awareness of His presence. Some have objected and said: No, what the church needs is: prayer warriors, evangelists, Bible teachers, missionaries, disciple-makers, etc. My response is: If we have a consciousness of God's presence, we will have all the above and more. How? Through obedience one is conscious of God's presence. Therefore, if we are conscious of His presence, we will obediently respond to His call with full assurance that He will provide all our needs for the tasks He assigns. He will provide all needs (in the local church) through His gifted servants.

Look at the promise of John 5:24:

> *John 5:24*
> *24 Verily, verily, I say unto you, He that heareth my word, and believeth on him that sent me, hath everlasting life, and shall not come into condemnation; but is passed from death unto life.*

The truth is undeniable! The Lord promises that eternal life is a present reality for those who obediently trust Him. It is only when we are in a state of obedience that He makes His presence known. It is similar to what Jesus told the woman at Jacob's well when He said that He had water to give her that would satisfy spiritual thirst forever (John 14:4). He was promising a present reality of eternal life.

The promise of Jesus is not an eternal life in the sweet-by-and-by, but right now in this present time of physical life.

We have only pulled back the veil and peeked into what Jesus taught about Eternal Life. The question is: Do you and I possess Eternal Life? It must be received as a gift. God has ordained to give it to only those who receive His Son.

Have you committed yourself to Christ and has Christ committed Himself to you?

Study Questions

1. What were the two cases cited concerning those who desired eternal life? What were the results and why?

2. What is the source of eternal life?

3. How do you know eternal life is a gift? How do you receive it?

4. How does having eternal life produce good works?

5. How is eternal life made a present reality?

CHAPTER 8

JESUS TAUGHT ABOUT
Abundant Life

Early in my pastoral ministry I came under the influence of the Keswick Convention. The convention was started in the eighteen-seventies in the village of Keswick, England. It has been meeting annually in the summer since its inception. Its original purpose was to seek spiritual renewal through an emphasis on the Holy Spirit in the lives of God's people.

It is a special interest gathering of evangelical Christians who wish to grow in grace by sensitizing themselves to the presence of God. It was through the influence of this convention's publications and audio cassettes that I began to understand that God wants His people to live **abundant** lives. Christian writer Ruth Paxson called it **Life on a Highest Plane**. Some have called it: The Exchanged Life,

The Victorious Life, The Spirit-Filled Life, The Surrendered Life, and The Sanctified Life. The Roman Catholic monk, Brother Lawrence, described it in his book titled *Practicing the Presence of God*. Regardless of what various Bible teachers have called this **abundant life**, it becomes apparent that there is one common truth connecting them all. The common truth is what Jesus taught His disciples.

How can we know what abundant life is like? Maybe the best way would be to discover what Jesus taught His disciples. Discovering the characteristics of such a life is only the first step. We must then learn how to adapt to those characteristics for everyday practical living. Why? So we may experience the abundant life. Therefore, we will observe the qualities Jesus taught. We will, under the leading of the Spirit, allow those qualities to conform us into His likeness.

Some of the truths we have already discovered will invariably be repeated again. Why? For two reasons: (1) because repetition was a teaching strategy the Lord used when sharing with His disciples and (2) spiritual truths have but one source that often overlap.

Consider the following.

Jesus Taught:
Abundant Life is a Promised Life

Look at John 7:37-39 where our Lord declared on the great Jewish feast day these words.

John 7:37-39

37 In the last day, that great day of the feast, Jesus stood and cried, saying, If any man thirst, let him come unto me, and drink.

38 He that believeth on me, as the scripture hath said, out of his belly shall flow rivers of living water.

39 (But this spake he of the Spirit, which they that believe on him should receive: for the Holy Ghost was not yet given; because that Jesus was not yet glorified.)

The *great day of the feast* in verse thirty-seven was the final day of the Feast of Tabernacles. It was celebrated at the Temple in Jerusalem. The apostle John wrote this account about 20 to 25 years after the Roman destruction of the temple in 70 AD. The destruction was caused by a political uprising of Jewish Zionist against Roman rule.

The feast was filled with spiritual lessons. God used the feast to remind Israel of His promises through the covenants with them. For example, one ceremony involved the daily fetching of water from the Pool of Siloam in a golden pitcher, and then a ritual pouring out of the water at the temple altar. The purpose was to remind the nation of God's miraculous provision of water while they were in the desert wilderness (Exodus 17:1–7; Numbers 20:1–11).

One of the symbols water represented was the presence of the Holy Spirit. Water is also seen as the Spirit cleansing His people and providing spiritual renewal through the various baptisms and ceremonial washings. All these ceremonies were pointing to the ministry of the Holy Spirit.

Thus, when Jesus stood and cried out His prophetic words, He was promising to quench thirst. He was referring to spiritual thirst that can only be met by the Spirit. The one person of the God-head that provides the resources for spiritual wholeness and abundant living is the Holy Spirit.

When the Lord spoke these words even the disciples did not fully comprehend them. What Jesus was talking about had never been experienced by anyone but Himself. His experience of the Spirit's indwelling presence would not be known by man until after His resurrection and ascension.

By the Spirit's indwelling presence Christ was promising a full and abundant life to all who would believe on and follow Him. It was in this manner that Jesus promised that believers could know the experience of an "abundant life."

Jesus Taught: Abundant Life is an Inclusive Life

The Abundant Life is a life promised to all believers who meet the conditions and is, therefore, inclusive.

> *John 10:1-10*
> *1 Verily, verily, I say unto you, He that entereth not by the door into the sheepfold, but climbeth up some other way, the same is a thief and a robber.*
> *2 But he that entereth in by the door is the shepherd of the sheep.*
> *3 To him the porter openeth; and the sheep hear his voice: and he calleth his own sheep by name, and leadeth them out.*

4 And when he putteth forth his own sheep, he goeth before them, and the sheep follow him: for they know his voice.

5 And a stranger will they not follow, but will flee from him: for they know not the voice of strangers.

6 This parable spake Jesus unto them: but they understood not what things they were which he spake unto them.

7 Then said Jesus unto them again, Verily, verily, I say unto you, I am the door of the sheep.

8 All that ever came before me are thieves and robbers: but the sheep did not hear them.

9 I am the door: by me if any man enter in, he shall be saved, and shall go in and out, and find pasture.

10 The thief cometh not, but for to steal, and to kill, and to destroy: I am come that they might have life, and that they might have it more abundantly.

In the parable above Jesus uses the analogy of a shepherd and his sheep to describe the relationship that Christians have with their Lord. As sheep know the shepherd's voice and follow him, so believers know the voice of their Shepherd and obey Him. The Abundant Life is not reserved for the spiritually elite. Every believer is included in the promise.

There are two qualifications: (1) hear His voice and (2) follow or obey Him. As we have already determined in the chapter on Eternal Life, the only ones who hear the voice of the Shepherd are those who have committed their souls to His keeping. Everyone who knows Him will spiritually hear Him. That principle is an inclusive constant.

No believer is excluded. There are, however, some conditions to a continual awareness of the Shepherd's presence. The first condition is obvious; one must be a genuine believer and not a pretender. The second is that the believer must be following the Shepherd in a moment-by-moment relationship.

Once willful disobedience enters the believer's life, the indwelling Spirit is grieved and He withdraws His fellowship (Ephesians 4:30). The believer then loses his sensitivity to the Shepherd's voice until he repents of his disobedience. The loss of sensitivity is one way the Father disciplines us and leads us into conviction. From conviction, He leads us to repentance and ultimately to restoration through forgiveness.

Jesus Taught:
Abundant Life is a Present Reality

John 11:21-27
21 Then said Martha unto Jesus, Lord, if thou hadst been here, my brother had not died.
22 But I know, that even now, whatsoever thou wilt ask of God, God will give it thee.
23 Jesus saith unto her, Thy brother shall rise again.
24 Martha saith unto him, I know that he shall rise again in the resurrection at the last day.
25 Jesus said unto her, I am the resurrection, and the life: he that believeth in me, though he were dead, yet shall he live:
26 And whosoever liveth and believeth in me shall never die. Believest thou this?

27 She saith unto him, Yea, Lord: I believe that thou art the Christ, the Son of God, which should come into the world.

Jesus uses the death of Lazarus to teach us about His authority and power over death. He is the source of life. He is spiritual life, and His life is an Abundant Life. We learn that physical life is a mirror image of spiritual life. I mean to say that we were born into a physical life that was marred by the presence of indwelling sin. Therefore, if we are to have real life (life from above), we must be born again into spiritual life. The spiritual life from God cannot sin. Why? Because, sin is not in His nature. It is not that we cannot sin. We can! But, when we do sin, it is caused by our not following the life-giving Spirit indwelling us. Sin comes when we follow the self life or sin nature of our physical birth called the flesh.

In the illustration above, Jesus shows His power over death by resurrecting Lazarus from physical death. His power over death illustrates His life giving power in both the physical and spiritual realms. Therefore, as Lazarus was raised from death physically, we who have trusted Christ have been raised from the dead spiritually. This is life that believers have done nothing to earn—it is a gift from God. You and I did nothing to obtain physical life, and we can do nothing to obtain spiritual life. All we can do is rejoice that He has awakened us. We now know who He is. He has given the gift that makes us alive right now! When He awakens you—to your sinful state and shows you what He has done to save you from your hopeless fate —all you can do is receive His gift by receiving His Son.

We learn from the apostle Paul that because of who we are in Christ and being alive through Him, we are given a special place in the heavens (Ephesians 1:3-6). It means that believers in Christ, at this very moment, are positioned in Christ and therefore are positionally with Him in heaven. Physically, we are still in this world but we are not of this world.

Jesus Taught:
Abundant Life is an Abiding Life

John 15:1-10
1 I am the true vine, and my Father is the husbandman.
2 Every branch in me that beareth not fruit he taketh away: and every branch that beareth fruit, he purgeth it, that it may bring forth more fruit.
3 Now ye are clean through the word which I have spoken unto you.
4 Abide in me, and I in you. As the branch cannot bear fruit of itself, except it abide in the vine; no more can ye, except ye abide in me.
5 I am the vine, ye are the branches: He that abideth in me, and I in him, the same bringeth forth much fruit: for without me ye can do nothing.
6 If a man abide not in me, he is cast forth as a branch, and is withered; and men gather them, and cast them into the fire, and they are burned.
7 If ye abide in me, and my words abide in you, ye shall ask what ye will, and it shall be done unto you.

*8 Herein is my Father glorified, that ye bear much
fruit; so shall ye be my disciples.
9 As the Father hath loved me, so have I loved
you: continue ye in my love.
10 If ye keep my commandments, ye shall abide in
my love; even as I have kept my Father's commandments, and abide in his love.*

The John 15 chapter has probably given believers more
hope and encouragement than most other passages. Why?
Because, in it we have described by the Lord the secret to
being a Spirit-filled Christian. By following the above
passage, believers are enabled to draw from the source of
power that provides and sustains life.

By studying the above passage we discover the three primary characteristics of living **abundantly**.

The first one is found in verse four where we find out that
the believer must **rest** in the vine. In the analogy, Jesus is
the vine; the branches that shoot out from the vine repre-
sent believers. The branches are to rest in the vine. What
does it mean to rest? Rest means to cease from labor or
activity. For example, a person may rest by sitting in a
chair. Here, the chair bears the weight that normally would
have been carried by the person himself. In the analogy
above we have the branches doing what is natural for the
branch—it rests in the vine. It makes no effort to be what
it is. It just is. The Christian is to rest in Christ and just be
who and what he is!

The second characteristic for abundant living is emphasized in verses four and five. The branch draws power
from the vine. The vine is the source from which the

branch draws its life. Fruit cannot grow on a branch that is not integrated with the vine. In like manner, the Christian is without a life source apart from Christ. Christ is our life! The abundant life is one that rests in the vine and draws its life from the vine while producing the fruit determined by the vine.

The abundant life can only be experienced when the believer is a fully functional and obedient member of the body of Christ and led by the Holy Spirit. As the believer draws strength and wisdom from the vine, he will spontaneously render a ministry in the name of the vine who is Christ.

The third characteristic is found in verse eight. Those who live the abundant life produce fruit. You may well ask what fruit? The answer depends on what the Master is doing in his life. Regardless of specifics, we do know this— the Spirit controlling him will produce His fruit in him. If he is controlled by the Holy Spirit, then he will produce the fruit of the Spirit that is: *love, joy, peace, patience, gentleness, goodness, faith, meekness, and temperance* (Galatians 5:22-23).

However, if he is controlled by the flesh (the indwelling sin nature) then he will produce the fruit of *adultery, fornication, uncleanness, lewdness, idolatry, sorcery, hatred, contentions, jealousies, outbursts of wrath, selfish ambitions, dissensions, heresies, envy, murders, drunkenness, revelries and such like these* (Galatians 5:19-21).

The Abundant Life is a life of spiritual rest or abiding, and spontaneously produces the fruit of Spirit in both attitude and action along with appropriate service as directed by God. There is more that could be said here but doing so would take us beyond the scope of our goal. If you are hungry for more about the abundant life, please read the works of Andrew Murray. I particularly commend his book on the Surrendered Life.

Jesus Taught:
The Abundant Life is a Joyful Life

John 15:11
[11] These things have I spoken unto you, that my joy might remain in you, and that your joy might be full.

Note the twofold desire for His disciples: (1) that His joy remains with us and (2) that His joy will fulfill us. The key to understanding is in the word joy. The Greek word for joy means the same as in English. It is an expression of a human attitude, or feeling caused by either a physical state or a particular hope. The Tyndall Bible Dictionary reminds us of three Scriptural examples of joy as a feeling: (1) the shepherd experienced joy when he found his lost sheep (Matthew 18:13) (2) the multitude felt joy when Jesus healed the woman who was bound by Satan for eighteen years (Luke 13:17) and (3) the disciples returned to the upper room rejoicing after witnessing Jesus ascend into the heavens (Acts 1:9-11).

Joy can also come as the result of a particular action. For example, Paul expressed his joy upon receiving news of Christians in Rome obeying God's truth (Romans 16:19). He also wrote to the Corinthians that we are not to rejoice in wrong but in righteousness or right actions (1 Corinthians 13:6). When the believer hears the truth—he rejoices in it—when he obeys the truth he rejoices in it! The Joyful Life is not one of giddy light-heartedness over frivolous occasions or events but rather is a life that rejoices in God and His glory.

Jesus Taught:
The Abundant Life is a Persecuted Life

John 15:19, 20
19 If ye were of the world, the world would love his own: but because ye are not of the world, but I have chosen you out of the world, therefore the world hateth you.
***20** Remember the word that I said unto you, The servant is not greater than his lord. If they have persecuted me, they will also persecute you; if they have kept my saying, they will keep yours also.*

Believers that have identified themselves with Christ can expect both love and hostility. Because you have aligned yourself with Him, you will be received by those who love Him and will be hated by those who despise Him.

The principle of **identification** is at the heart of New Testament Christianity. When we believe God's message and are born from above, we are baptized by the Holy Spirit into a spiritual body called **the body of Christ**. From that point forward we are warmly drawn to others who are like us. We have common ground in our relationship with Christ.

We find ourselves having a new and fresh understanding of the Word. Where we were formerly disobedient and defiant, we now find that we agree with God and judge ourselves taking a stand with Him against our own sins. Such new sensitivities as these are common among those who have found new life in Him and have identified with Him.

Our identification with Christ propels us into three realities: (1) purpose, (2) philosophy and (3) worldview. Because we are one with Christ, we have become one with Him in everything that the Father sets forth.

His purpose has become our purpose. Jesus came to restore glory to His Father by destroying sin and its power. It was sin that originally tainted God's glory. Jesus prayed in John 17 that He again would know the glory He and His Father experienced in eternity past. We are extensions of our Lord's purpose and are actively engaged in bringing to pass His ultimate goal of restoring His glory. In eternity future, there will be no sin and God's glory will abound.

His philosophy becomes our philosophy. Jesus' philosophy was to finish the thinking and processes set in motion by His Father. As disciples of Christ we extend the Father's thinking by submitting to the mind of Christ. Paul said, *Let this mind be in you; which was also in Christ Jesus* (Philippians 2:5). As offensive as it may sound to our flesh we are slaves to the will of God. The difference in the people of the world and the Christian is the master being served. The servants of sin are enslaved by its lusts. Those enslaved by God's love are free to serve righteousness.

We turn to the subject of worldview and ask: What should be our view of the world? The Christian worldview is determined by the revelation of God's Word. We view the world through God's eyes. The world calls evil good, and we look into God's Word and determine that evil is not good but is an abomination. Therefore, we agree with God. Why, because when the Bible tells us that we are sinners, we look at ourselves and see that we are indeed sinners. Therefore, in identifying ourselves with God, we are determined to follow Him, think like Him, and see things the way He sees them.

It should be well established in your mind—believers may expect the same treatment from the world as Jesus received. Why? Because we are at one in purpose, in philosophy, and hold the same worldview as our Savior.

Jesus Taught:
The Abundant Life is a Witnessing Life

John 15:26-27
26 But when the Comforter is come, whom I will send unto you from the Father, even the Spirit of truth, which proceedeth from the Father, he shall testify of me:
27 And ye also shall bear witness, because ye have been with me from the beginning.

When Jesus spoke these words He directed them to His apostles. They were the very ones who had accompanied Him in His earthly ministry. These disciples had received the investment of Jesus' life into their own. He was part of them and bonded with them as a man. He would later deepen His bond spiritually.

In this prophetical statement, He told them what they would become when they received the indwelling gift of the Holy Spirit's presence (John 20:21). He shared what would become their life's goal. It was not what they would do but what they would be—witnesses to the Father's absolute truth. Not only will these apostles be witnesses in the world, but all who believe them will also take up the testimony of the cross. God will raise up faithful witnesses unto Himself out of every successive generation.

Think with me about what the witnesses will not be. Focusing on what we are not will accentuate what we are.

God's people will not be self-righteous in their witness. Christians who are walking in God's light do not talk down to people as if they were superior or were particularly entitled because of their own goodness. A Christian witness is offered with a sense of unworthiness and humility. Why? Because the closer one gets to God the more he realizes his own sinfulness, while simultaneously experiencing a sense of acceptance and affirmation.

Humility is the hallmark of being an effective witness to the glory of God. We know that we were purchased with a price—a price we could not pay on our own behalf. We were sinners condemned and destined for the eternal lake of fire. Because of Christ's death on Calvary, God directed our faith to what Christ has done on our behalf. Then, in grace, He plucked us as a branding iron from the flames of Hell fire—a fire reserved for the Devil and his fallen angels.

A proper witness for God is shown by the attitude and spirit expressed in the old Gospel hymn by William R. Newell—

AT CALVARY
Lyrics by William R. Newell

Years I spent in vanity and pride,
Caring not my Lord was crucified,
Knowing not it was for me He died
On Calvary.

By God's Word at last my sin I learned;
Then I trembled at the law I'd spurned,
Till my guilty soul imploring turned
To Calvary.

Now I've giv'n to Jesus everything,
Now I gladly own Him as my King,
Now my raptured soul can only sing
Of Calvary!

Oh, the love that drew salvation's plan!
Oh, the grace that brought it down to man!
Oh, the mighty gulf that God did span
At Calvary!

Refrain:
Mercy there was great, and grace was free;
Pardon there was multiplied to me;
There my burdened soul found liberty
At Calvary.

Another witnessing negative is this: the Christian does not witness in his own strength. Jesus informed His disciples

140

that He was the vine, and they were the branches. Thus, as the branch draws strength from the vine to bear its fruit, the believer draws strength from the indwelling Spirit to bear a testimony about Christ's dying for the sins of the world, and God granting grace to all who believes on or commits to Christ as the saving Lord.

The witnessing life is a life that witnesses to what it is. It does not try to be a witness. What he is flows naturally and spontaneously from his life. Such a life does not work at what it is—it just is. Be who you are in Christ and give the Father glory by sharing the good news.

The resurrection of Jesus Christ has assured an abundant life for all who trust Him. Our acceptance before God our Father rests absolutely on the substitutionary death and resurrection of Jesus Christ. **If you are not enjoying the Abundant Life, it is because you have neglected your relationship with Him.**

Study Guide

1. On what basis can we say that Jesus taught that the Abundant Life is promised?

2. What does the word **inclusive** mean as it relates to the Abundant Life?

3. How does abiding in Christ produce the Abundant Life?

4. Why is the Abundant Life subject to persecution?

5. One who witnesses to God's truth out of an abundant

6. life does not exhibit self-righteousness. Why?

CHAPTER 9

WHAT JESUS TAUGHT ABOUT DISCIPLESHIP

Jesus was the ultimate disciple of His father. He said this: *. . . I say unto you, The Son can do nothing of himself, but what he seeth the Father do: for what things soever he doeth, these also doeth the Son likewise* (John 5:19).

If we can determine the characteristics of Jesus following His Father, then we will begin to understand the nature of discipleship and mentoring. Knowing these characteristics will guide us in knowing what to teach the church. The Bible does not provide us with a technical definition for discipleship. But, the Scriptures do give us numerous illustrations of what discipleship will look like when practiced.

Empirically, we may look to our culture and find numerous examples of secular discipleship. For example, when Lee Iacocca was instrumental in turning the Chrysler Corporation from the brink of bankruptcy, it was common to find industrial executives who became his disciples. It is not uncommon to find students who mimic their teachers, or children who mimic their parents. When children become teenagers, we often observe them dressing and adopting behavior like their heroes and heroines. Therefore, it is easy to see that disciples are followers.

Jesus Taught:
Discipleship is Identification with Christ

In the spiritual realm, disciples are followers of Christ. We need to learn to follow Christ not for a particular time but for life. Let us look at what Jesus taught:

> *Matthew 10:32-39*
> *32 Whosoever therefore shall confess me before men, him will I confess also before my Father which is in heaven.*
> *33 But whosoever shall deny me before men, him will I also deny before my Father which is in heaven.*
> *34 Think not that I am come to send peace on earth: I came not to send peace, but a sword.*
> *35 For I am come to set a man at variance against his father, and the daughter against her mother, and the daughter in law against her mother in law.*

146

36 And a man's foes shall be they of his own household.
37 He that loveth father or mother more than me is not worthy of me: and he that loveth son or daughter more than me is not worthy of me.
38 And he that taketh not his cross, and followeth after me, is not worthy of me.
39 He that findeth his life shall lose it: and he that loseth his life for my sake shall find it.

Upon reading the above passage, one undeniable characteristic is apparent. Jesus demands that everyone take a position of either being for or against Him! Those who identify with Him will be received by His Father. Those who refuse, will be denied by Jesus before the Father. The statement echoes the words of the apostle John in his Gospel where he declares that people are separated from God because they do not believe on the Son (John3:18).

The question is often debated whether one can be a believer and choose or choose not to be a disciple. It appears that to identify with the Son is to be His disciple and to discipline yourself to follow Him.

You may well ask: What does it mean to identify with someone? From the passage above, there are at least four ways a person can be identified with another:

(1) Identification through purpose (verses 32, 33)— when you bond with a person, to the extent that you take on his purposes in life, you have truly identified with him. It is in this way that we are to identify and bond with Christ. His purposes are to be our purposes.

(2) Identification through warfare (verses 34-36)—when identified with another, you take on that person's battles. You become an ally against a common enemy. Therefore, being identified with Christ we become the enemies of the world, the flesh, and the Devil.

(3) Identification through love (verses 37, 38)—when you commit yourself to someone, you declare your love through allegiance. Love is not primarily an emotion. It is better understood by action. In these particular verses real love is seen as contrasted with hate. Jesus is not saying that we are to hate our family. I believe that He is saying, our love for Him is to be so strong that when compared to family it would be as hate.

(4) Identification through obedience (verse 39)—when you do something for someone because of love, you identify with them. Jesus said His sheep hear His voice and obey Him. Through obedience the Christian shows his identification with the Son and the Father. He does so in the power of the Spirit.

Jesus Taught: Discipleship is Communing with the Father

Communing with God requires time and spiritual focus. The Holy Scriptures provide us with God's only instruction about how to know Him, relate to Him, communion with Him and draw near to Him. The Son of man sets the example:

Matthew 17-19
17 Now the first day of the feast of unleavened
bread the disciples came to Jesus, saying unto

*him, Where wilt thou that we prepare for thee to
eat the passover?*
*18 And he said, Go into the city to such a man,
and say unto him, The Master saith, My time is at
hand; I will keep the passover at thy house with
my disciples.*
*19 And the disciples did as Jesus had appointed
them; and they made ready the passover.*

The Passover feast was a sacred meal, celebrating the deliverance of Israel from the bondage of Egypt. It is recorded in Exodus 12:3-10. The history behind the Passover is significant. One of the ten plagues upon Egypt was the death of the first born of every family and beast in Egypt. The only exception would be the families of Israel that prepared a sacrificial lamb, marked their door posts with its blood, cooked the lamb in a prescribed manner, and ate it. Its remains were to be consumed by fire.

When the death angel passed through Egypt, the first born of every household was killed. The messenger of death passed over the homes of the Israelites whose doors were marked by the blood of the lamb. So great was the grief in Egypt that pharaoh agreed to let God's people go.

The Jewish people celebrate that historic release from Egyptian tyranny every year. It has become a time of communion with God out of gratefulness for His saving them from the Egyptian bondage. In all probability, Jesus, up to the time of His baptism by John, had celebrated the Passover with his family. Since then, He was with His disciples.

Now, on this final occasion, He draws His disciples around Him and begins again to explain His death. On previous occasions, when He had sought to prepare them for what was coming, they were in a state of denial.[2] But, on this occasion, as Jesus began to speak there were only eager hearers. While all He said is not recorded, they were informed that one of their very number would betray Him, He would die, and then after three days rise again.

As He began the meal, He took the bread and blessed it and said, *Take, eat; this is my body.* (Matthew 26:26) *He then took the cup, blessed it, and said, "Drink ye all of it; For this is my blood of the new testament, which is shed for many for the remission of sins.* (Matthew 26:27, 28) They sang a hymn and left that upper room.

Jesus entered the garden to pray. He bid His disciples to pray as He went deeper into the garden. He wished to privately commune with His Father. In this private place, He asked the Father to remove the cup of torment from Him. Nevertheless, Jesus submitted to the will of the Father. As a man, it may be that Jesus did not want to go through the agony of suffering for sin and the rejection of His Father. As the divine Son of God, He resolutely determined to submit Himself to the will of His Father—a will that had been set in eternity past. Jesus was born to die for the sins of the world!

In the history of mankind, there likely has never been communion with the Father that would equal that of Jesus' experience in the garden of Gethsemane. But it is that kind

---

[2] Peter went so far as to rebuke Jesus for sharing such unthinkable things (Matthew 16:23). Jesus answered him and said that he was full of the thoughts of the adversary—Satan.

of communion that will infuse Christian discipleship with the power needed to do His work in a fallen world.

Regular communion with the Father is a necessity for maintenance of the disciple's spiritual life.

Jesus Taught:
Discipleship is Bearing His Cross

Earlier in His ministry Jesus had begun to prepare His apostles for training other disciples. His teaching included an explanation of what would be necessary to be counted a disciple of Jesus.

> *Matthew 16:24, 25*
> *24 Then said Jesus unto his disciples, If any man will come after me, let him deny himself, and take up his cross, and follow me.*
> *25 For whosoever will save his life shall lose it: and whosoever will lose his life for my sake shall find it.*

The three elements of Christian discipleship are: (1) denial of self, (2) taking up the cross, and (3) following Christ. Let us consider each of these elements in their order. Do not think that the order is arbitrary. The Word of God is precise in its use of words, concepts, truths, and information presented. Therefore, when the Lord presents a principle to be followed, it is likely that key information might have proceeded it in the order of His revelation.

The first order of Christian discipleship is the denial of self. When we first come to Christ, we are caught up in the euphoria of being saved. We experience freedom from the bondage of sin and a sense of forgiveness from God. We begin a life of anticipation. We begin thinking about the great reward of eternal life now and in heaven with God and His holy angels. However, while all that is true, there is a war being waged that engages us when we come to Christ. It is a war of which many Christians are unaware. Why? Because, believers often assume things that are not true. Some have thought that, after receiving Christ, life would be as a "walk in the park." When in reality, they found the Christian life is far more challenging than life as a sinner.

Jesus commanded His disciples to put first things first. He asked for his disciples to first give up their personal rights. He asked them to transfer rights of ownership. He said it something like this: *if you want to save your life you must lose it.* From the Biblical perspective denial of self is putting the will of God before your own.

When Jesus called His first disciples who became His apostles, He asked them to give up their vocations—leave their homes and families—devote themselves to Him. Every succeeding generation of believers has received the same call. In the same way He called His first apostles, He is still calling today. While relatively few are called to professional ministry, all are called to the ministry of serving Him. All are called to a life of denying self!

What does denying self look like? You may see it in the garden of Gethsemane, where Jesus surrendered His will to His Father, as He contemplated the agony He must suffer for the sins of the world. You also may see it in the lives of the Apostles, who gave themselves for the testimony of Christ counting their own lives as nothing compared to God's truth. Down through the centuries, God's people have been counting the cost of serving Him at the expense of serving self.

God does not call all His people to be pastors, teachers, missionaries, or other professional ministries. But, He does call all to a life of self-denial. Every act must be in submission to the Lord Jesus. God cares about every decision you make—what you wear—how you wear it—what you drive—where you play—who you hang with—from whom you seek advice—just to mention a few. God wants to be the first one consulted! When you come to Christ, you are under new management. If not, something is wrong!

In the words of Issac Watt's hymn, When I Survey the Wondrous Cross, we find the proper attitude of one who loses his life to save it.

When I Survey the Wondrous Cross
by Sir Issac Watts

When I survey the wondrous cross
on which the Prince of Glory died;
my richest gain I count but loss,
and pour contempt on all my pride.

Forbid it, Lord, that I should boast,
save in the death of Christ, my God;
all the vain things that charm me most,
I sacrifice them to his blood.

See, from his head, his hands, his feet,
sorrow and love flow mingled down.
Did e'er such love and sorrow meet,

or thorns compose so rich a crown.

Were the whole realm of nature mine,
that were an offering far too small;
love so amazing, so divine,
demands my soul, my life, my all.

The second prong of Christian discipleship is taking up the cross. Here, we have another aspect of Biblical Christianity that is often misunderstood.

On one occasion, I was making a pastoral visit to the hospital. The lady I was visiting had a reputation for being a sincere believer. I believe her reputation was an accurate one. She appeared to truly love the Lord. As I was concluding my visit, I offered to pray with her and somehow the subject of her illness became the topic of our conversation. She referred to her illness as her cross. She thought she was bearing her illness as a cross for Christ. I prayed and departed. Her thinking on what it means to bear a cross was faulty. It was not the time or place to correct her theology about personal illness.

This chapter is the time!

When Christ told His disciples, they were to take up their cross, He was talking about identification with God. It was to be an identification that affects the entirety of one's life.

Look with me at the system that condemned and crucified Christ. When the Roman justice system was in full swing, those being condemned as criminals, left the judgment hall and took up their cross on the way to the crucifixion site. In just that way Jesus carried His cross to His death.

The Lord is saying take up your cross of death to self and bear it in identification with Me.

You and I must be willing to take up our cross in identification with Christ. We are to so identify with Him that the world's hatred for Him will be directed to us. Despite what they say or what they threaten to do, we must not abandon the cross of our testimony.

This year, 2015, about twenty Egyptian Christians lost their lives just because they were Christians—because they would not deny their faith. We are told they were beheaded in a merciless fashion.

Disciple of Christ, take up your cross! Identify yourself with Him and take upon yourself His reproach. Rejoice in His victories, but in the world, you will suffer persecution. Remember, if the world hates Him, it will hate you.

The third prong of discipleship is following Christ. While we continue to live a life of self-denial, we must continue our identification with Him by bearing the cross of His reproach. Now, moment by moment we must follow Him.

The only way to follow Him is to know Him. We cannot know Him without spending time with Him in communion through the study of His word and prayer. Our knowledge of Him is directly related to the quality time spent with Him. His Word reveals Him that you may know Him. His thoughts and desires are shared in the Word. His will is not a mystery kept only for the spiritual elite.

As we invest time with Him, we develop a sensitivity to His voice and we follow Him like the sheep we are. Following Jesus is as simple as trusting what He says and obeying Him.

For further study read the following passages: Mathew 16:24; Mark 8:34; Luke 9:23; Luke 14:27.

Study Guide

1. What does it mean to be identified with Christ?

2. How does one commune with God? Explain!

3. Describe what it means to bear your cross.

CHAPTER 10

WHAT JESUS TAUGHT ABOUT HELL

It is commonly thought that Jesus spoke more about love than any other subject. However, a closer look will reveal that He spent a major portion of His time teaching and warning about judgment and hell. In this section, our purpose is to observe what Jesus really taught and draw the appropriate conclusions.

Some have concluded that because God is loving, there is no such thing as a place of torment or judgment. Truth is —God is love, and because of His love, there is no allowance for the violation of His other attributes such as holiness, righteousness, and justice. All in His presence must be as He is. Therefore, no sin or anyone tainted by sin can enter the presence of God.

Jesus Taught:
Hell is a Place to Avoid

We will begin with what Jesus said in Matthew 5:

Matthew 5:22-30
22 But I say unto you, That whosoever is angry with his brother without a cause shall be in danger of the judgment: and whosoever shall say to his brother, Raca, shall be in danger of the council: but whosoever shall say, Thou fool, shall be in danger of hell fire.
23 Therefore if thou bring thy gift to the altar, and there rememberest that thy brother hath ought against thee;
24 Leave there thy gift before the altar, and go thy way; first be reconciled to thy brother, and then come and offer thy gift.
25 Agree with thine adversary quickly, whiles thou art in the way with him; lest at any time the adversary deliver thee to the judge, and the judge deliver thee to the officer, and thou be cast into prison.
26 Verily I say unto thee, Thou shalt by no means come out thence, till thou hast paid the uttermost farthing.
27 Ye have heard that it was said by them of old time, Thou shalt not commit adultery:

28 But I say unto you, That whosoever looketh on a woman to lust after her hath committed adultery with her already in his heart.
29 And if thy right eye offend thee, pluck it out, and cast it from thee: for it is profitable for thee that one of thy members should perish, and not that thy whole body should be cast into hell.
30 And if thy right hand offend thee, cut it off, and cast it from thee: for it is profitable for thee that one of thy members should perish, and not that thy whole body should be cast into hell.

Jesus taught Hell was a place to avoid by calling attention to attitudes and actions that may cause a person to be a candidate for the place of torment.

We must remember the context of Jesus' teaching. He was delivering a message often called The Sermon on the Mount. Jesus' ministry was primarily to the lost sheep of the house of Israel. The people that gathered around Him were primarily those who considered themselves accept-able to God because of their adherence to the Law, and the temple worship. They followed the teachings of the priests and offered the appropriate blood sacrifices. Therefore, much of His ethical teaching mirrored the heart of His Fa-ther.

Through the Commandments given to Moses, God had revealed His moral character and demanded His people be holy as He was holy. My personal conviction is that the sermon on the mountain side in Galilee was Jesus' com-mentary on the Ten Commandments. In it, He emphasizes that keeping the Law of God begins in the heart. It appears the teachers of Israel had so reinterpreted the meaning of the Law that it had become a matter of physical action only. The motives of the heart were not considered in their interpretation. Jesus corrects this by showing them that God is first concerned with the motive of the heart and then the obedience of the body. He shows that what is in our hearts will be revealed through the activity of our lives.

When we look at what Jesus taught on this occasion, we begin to realize how hopeless we are without the mercy and grace of God through Christ. At this specific time in history, Jesus had not revealed Himself as the Lamb of God. John, the baptizer, had declared Him to be so. He made this declaration just before Jesus was baptized and the official launch of His earthly ministry. However, few understood the proclamation. They would not understand until after His resurrection. Only then would they recognize that Jesus truly was the Son of God. Who He is and what He had done would begin to dawn upon them.

By implication, Hell is a place to be avoided because it is a place of punishment. Jesus provides some illustrations that remind us of how easily our actions can endanger us as candidates for torment. For example, He cites calling people derogatory names like Raca or empty-headed will put you in danger of being censored by the authorities and even jailed. If you call a person a "fool," you are in danger of being cast into Hell or the fires of torment. Those to whom He was speaking would have understood the illustration as a reference to the valley of Hinnom or valley of destruction. Hinnom was the name of a valley just outside the Southern wall of Jerusalem where pagans in previous centuries had offered human sacrifices. In Jesus' day, it was a place of continual fire where refuse was burned.

Fire and smoke rose from the valley night and day. It provided a good illustration of the lake of fire referenced in Mark's Gospel (Mark 9:44).

Jesus was saying that the Father's standard was not as had been supposed. He illustrated how the Father looks at a man's heart. He gave two examples to show how God judges man . In the first He said that if one were guilty of being angry without a righteous cause, he was guilty of murder (Matthew 5:22). He also said that if a man looks on a woman with lust in his heart, that same man is guilty of adultery (Matthew 5:28).

Using the above illustrations of anger and adultery, Jesus shows that all mankind stands before God guilty of sin and deserving of Hell. The smallest or what we might consider the most insignificant sin makes us unfit for Heaven and only fit for Hell. Why? Because, only the pure of heart can go to Heaven. (See chapter one for a clearer understanding of why all people need God's provision for personal salvation.)

Space does not permit us a fuller exposition of the Matthew 5:22-30 passage. I believe we have served the purpose of showing that Hell is a place to be avoided. Why? Because, it is the proverbial garbage heap of sinful beings and sin.

Jesus Taught:
Hell is a Destination

Hell is a specific place. Consider the following verses.

Matthew 11:23, 24

163

23 And thou, Capernaum, which art exalted unto heaven, shalt be brought down to hell: for if the mighty works, which have been done in thee, had been done in Sodom, it would have remained until this day.
24 But I say unto you, That it shall be more tolerable for the land of Sodom in the day of judgment, than for thee.

Jesus compared Capernaum to Sodom. He said that Sodom would fair better than Capernaum on the day of judgment. Sodom was a wicked city that had existed during the time of Abraham and Lot. Abraham had given Lot his choice of pasture land, and he had chosen the Jordan Valley near Sodom. The city had become known for its sexual perversion. Lot had risen to a position of leadership. His time in Sodom was vexing to him. Peter said that Lot was a "righteous soul" (2 Peter 2:8). The city became so wicked that God sent angels to usher Lot and his family out prior to destroying it.

Capernaum was a fishing village on the North shore of Galilee. Jesus had spent much time—taught in the synagogue there—performed miracles of healing and other ministries that bore testimony showing who He was. The city's general population rejected Christ and His witness—that He was the Son of God. It was for this reason that Jesus judged Capernaum. The most serious of all sins is the rejection of Christ! Why? Because, when one rejects Christ, he has rejected the only one through whom God can save him.

Jesus appoints Hell as the final destination of Capernaum. By making such a statement, He shows us that Hell is a place. Comparatively, Capernaum was a morally good city. Preachers have unsuccessfully tried to share that people do not go to Hell for sins so much as the rejection of God's message (Romans 1:8-21). Why? Because, all men are sinners when they come into the world—they do not become sinners by sinning. Sinners are born in that state (Romans 3:10, 23). It was so with Capernaum and will be so with all who follow Capernaum's example of rejecting the witness of God.

Hell is a real place of destination into which all souls are rushing who have rejected God's testimony.

Jesus Taught:
Hell is a Place of Destruction

Matthew 10:28
And fear not them which kill the body, but are not able to kill the soul: but rather fear him which is able to destroy both soul and body in hell.

The verse above is the testimony of Jesus, that Hell is a literal place and is a place of destruction. Destruction does not necessarily mean annihilation. In numerous New Testament references "Hell" is described as an everlasting punishment of pain and isolation from the love and mercy of God. We use the word destruction to show that the sinner's life is finally destroyed in the fiery wasteland of Hell and is not consumed (Mark 9:43, 44).

The idea of an eternal place of punishment was alluded to as early as the writings of Moses in the Pentateuch. It was directly spoken of in the Psalms and the Prophets. However a full revelation of eternal punishment is not understood until we come to the witness of the New Testament writers who received their knowledge directly from Jesus.

Here are the facts about Hell:

(1) is a literal place (Matthew 11:23);

(2) is a place of eternal torment (Luke 16:23);

(3) is a place of intense fire (Mark 9:43);

(4) is a place of utter darkness (2 Peter2:4);

(5) is a place of consciousness (Luke 16:19-31).

There are many who want to know: Why would a loving and caring God allow punishment to continue eternally? They seem to think that the crime does not fit the punishment. Such thoughts can only come from people who do not understand the true nature of sin and unrighteousness. A man easily dismisses sin because he sees sin as no big deal. However, God is pure and Holy and will not—no, cannot allow sin in His presence! Therefore, all in rebellion against Him, will receive in punishment the mirror image of the eternal bliss of those in Heaven. If His blessings continue forever, why should not His punishment continue forever? The testimony of Scripture is that it will!

Jesus Taught:
Hell is a Place of Consciousness

Consider carefully Luke 16:19-31.

Luke 16:19-31

19 There was a certain rich man, which was clothed in purple and fine linen, and fared sumptuously every day:

20 And there was a certain beggar named Lazarus, which was laid at his gate, full of sores,

21 And desiring to be fed with the crumbs which fell from the rich man's table: moreover the dogs came and licked his sores.

22 And it came to pass, that the beggar died, and was carried by the angels into Abraham's bosom: the rich man also died, and was buried;

23 And in hell he lift up his eyes, being in torments, and seeth Abraham afar off, and Lazarus in his bosom.

24 And he cried and said, Father Abraham, have mercy on me, and send Lazarus, that he may dip the tip of his finger in water, and cool my tongue; for I am tormented in this flame.

25 But Abraham said, Son, remember that thou in thy lifetime receivedst thy good things, and likewise Lazarus evil things: but now he is comforted, and thou art tormented.

26 And beside all this, between us and you there is a great gulf fixed: so that they which would pass from hence to you cannot; neither can they pass to us, that would come from thence.

27 Then he said, I pray thee therefore, father, that thou wouldest send him to my father's house:

28 For I have five brethren; that he may testify unto them, lest they also come into this place of torment.

29 Abraham saith unto him, They have Moses and the prophets; let them hear them.

*30 And he said, Nay, father Abraham: but if one
went unto them from the dead, they will repent.
31 And he said unto him, If they hear not Moses
and the prophets, neither will they be persuaded,
though one rose from the dead.*

In simple language Jesus tells us the story of a rich man and Lazarus. The story is thought by some to be a parable. Others believe it was the telling of a historical case. The latter has one fact going for it—no other parable identifies a person by providing a name. Therefore, we believe this to be an account of historical reality.

The poor man's name is Lazarus. We know nothing else about him, except he was so poor that he sought the crumbs from the rich man's table. He had sores that may indicate he was in a state of poor nutrition. Lazarus died and was received by the Lord. The term "Abraham's bosom" is a Hebrew idiom referring to God the Father.

The rich man, who's name is not provided, dies and awakens in Hell. From the account, we may glean the following facts.

(1) *And in hell he lift up his eyes,*—Hell is a physical place holding a representation of his physical body (awaiting the resurrection)—we know this because he could see.

(2) *. . .being in torments. . .,*—Hell is a place of torment!

(3) *And in hell he lift up his eyes, being in torments, and seeth Abraham afar off, and Lazarus in his bosom.*—In Hell, one will be conscious of the reality of Heaven.

(4) *. . .have mercy on me, and send Lazarus*,—The physical senses of touch and feel will be an active realization. We know this because the rich man made an appeal to God that Lazarus be allowed to come and alleviate his pain.

(5) *Son, remember that thou in thy lifetime receivedst thy good things, and likewise Lazarus evil things: but now he is comforted, and thou art tormented.* —In Hell one will be aware of why he is there. (Judgment is based on a person's works. Therefore, because all are sinners, all will be sent to Hell unless they respond to God in faith, believing His message of hope.)

(6) *between us and you there is a great gulf fixed:*— There is a great gulf between Heaven and Hell and no transitions are allowed from one to the other. We are not told the nature of the gulf.

(7) *Then he said, I pray thee therefore, father, that thou wouldest send him to my father's house:*—In Hell there will be no answers to prayer. The rich man had five brothers, whom he wanted Lazarus to warn about the reality of Hell.

(8) *Abraham saith unto him, They have Moses and the prophets; let them hear them. 30 And he said, Nay, father Abraham: but if one went unto them from the dead, they will repent.*—In Hell, man's thinking is still faulty, the rich man thinks that if Lazarus is resurrected and sent to his brothers they will repent. God, knowing the hearts of men, declares . . .*If they hear not Moses and the prophets, neither will they be persuaded, though one rose*

from the dead. A man believes what his heart wants to believe!

The rich man and all who follow their own rebellious sin nature will ultimately end up in Hell—a place of keen consciousness and sorrow—alienated from God's love and mercy forever and ever. However, it does not have to be so. God is faithful and merciful. He promises to save all who will come to Him believing on the finished work of Christ on Calvary.

Study Guide

1. How do you know that Hell is a real place?

2. What evidence do we have that Hell is a place of torment?

3.According to the writer—what are the eight things that can be learned from Luke 16:19-31?

4. How do we know that the soul is not annihilated in Hell?

CHAPTER 11

WHAT JESUS TAUGHT
About Heaven

Mankind has been plagued for thousands of generations about the source of life. It has vexed him ever since he lost his awareness of God's identity. Because man inherently knows that God exists, he is prone to try to worship Him. But, not willing to accept God's revelation of Himself and how He is to be worshipped, man began creating his own gods and designing his own worship. A man makes his god in the likeness of created things; for example, the sun, moon, eagle, bull, serpent, etc. These gods created by man may have had the image of a created thing, but the god it represented was actually nothing more than what man wanted his god to be.

His intuitive knowledge that he had a creator—to whom he ultimately would have to give an account—caused him to seek a process of appeasement with his god. It began with Cain and continues to this day. Because of man's sin, it appears that the possibility for man's worship to become perverted increased the further removed he was from his experience in Eden.

When in seminary, I was assigned the task of writing a paper on the ancient religions. As I studied, several things became apparent. One was the fact that many of the major religions have a flood account in their history. I asked myself how would one explain this? I concluded that if all religions came from the same source—that is, God originally provided instructions for acceptable worship—then it would naturally follow that there would be some common elements in their histories. There was only one true manner of worship that was provided in the garden in Eden. Then, after the destruction of the world-wide flood, Noah instituted true worship as instructed by God.

As man multiplied and replenished the earth, their rebellious nature (inherited from Adam) caused them to pervert the true religion taught of their fathers. For example, the logical procession would have been for Noah to teach his family all he knew about God and how to worship Him. Included in Noah's instructions would have been the insight he had received from God about a place of blessing for the faithful and a place of torment for the disobedient. Although God has always had a remnant of faithful people, the further in time man is removed from Noah's instruction, the greater the possibilities for perverted worship. Ultimately, worship can only happen when man honors God according to God's revelation of Himself through Jesus the Christ.

There was not a highly developed concept of heaven in the Old Testament. The promises of God to His people were primarily related to a promised place of habitation on earth—the increase in their nation's population and physical prosperity. Heaven and Hell were alluded to but not emphasized as in the New Testament. Over the centuries the Jewish rabbis would record their interpretations of the Scripture and would develop a system of theological concepts. By the time Christ came, there were three primary religious sects among the Jews. These were the Pharisees, the Sadducees and the Essenes. These theological sects and systems of interpretation can be historically traced to around 200-150 BC.

The Pharisees were very literal in understanding spiritual things. For example, they believed in a literal resurrection for mankind. They also believed in both Heaven and Hell. However, the Sadducees did not believe in a resurrection to an afterlife nor did they believe in angels. It is reported that the only part of the Bible they accepted was the Pentateuch or the books of Moses. Generally, the Sadducees were of the wealthy class and the Pharisees were of the common people.

The Essenes were likely a sect that split from the Pharisees or from the Hasidim as they were once called. They were very spiritual in their emphasis on religion and had a three year initiation rite. To my knowledge Jesus never mentions the Essenes.

This was the religious and historical backdrop against which Jesus teaches us about the afterlife of the believer.

We will look at what Jesus taught in the Gospels and then at what can be learned from Jesus' revelation of the future as recorded by the apostle John. Our goal is to get a grasp of Jesus' general teaching about Heaven.

Jesus Taught:
Heaven is a Kingdom

The first record of Jesus' mentioning heaven is after His baptism by John. While the timeline is not clear, it appears, that He returned from Judea to His home in Nazareth. Then, because of John the Baptist's arrest, He retreated from Nazareth and went to Capernaum and made the upper region of Galilee His home base. We are not certain why John's arrest would have triggered such a move.

We have His first reference to Heaven in Matthew 4:17.

> *Matthew 4:17*
> *17 "From that time Jesus began to preach, and to say, Repent: for the kingdom of heaven is at hand."*

By making this statement, Jesus was confirming that Heaven was a real place and that God is its King. By implication, He was also saying that He was in the world to complete Heaven's mission. There is also a sense in which He is the embodiment of the Kingdom of Heaven.

A kingdom has a realm over which a king reigns. We know from other studies that the King is the triune God,

Father, Son, and Holy Spirit. The location of the Kingdom is not mentioned in this reference, but from other passages we know that three heavens are referenced in Scripture. The earth's atmosphere is the first heaven; outer space, where the solar systems and galaxies reside is the second heaven; the third heaven is beyond the first two and it is known to be the residence of God and the seat of His Kingdom.

Jesus Taught:
Heaven's Residents Have
Certain Characteristics

Moving on to what is titled The Sermon on the Mount, we discover several characteristics about the residents of Heaven.

> *Matthew 5:2-12*
> *2 And he opened his mouth, and taught them, saying,*
> *3 Blessed are the poor in spirit: for theirs is the kingdom of heaven.*
> *4 Blessed are they that mourn: for they shall be comforted.*
> *5 Blessed are the meek: for they shall inherit the earth.*
> *6 Blessed are they which do hunger and thirst after righteousness: for they shall be filled.*
> *7 Blessed are the merciful: for they shall obtain mercy.*
> *8 Blessed are the pure in heart: for they shall see God.*

9 Blessed are the peacemakers: for they shall be called the children of God.

10 Blessed are they which are persecuted for righteousness' sake: for theirs is the kingdom of heaven.

11 Blessed are ye, when men shall revile you, and persecute you, and shall say all manner of evil against you falsely, for my sake.

12 Rejoice, and be exceeding glad: for great is your reward in heaven: for so persecuted they the prophets which were before you.

Among those who reside in Heaven will be *the poor in spirit*, and *the persecuted for righteousness sake*. While these verses are addressed to the Jews, the message is transcultural and is applicable to all God's people.

Who are the poor in spirit? Generally, the Greek word for poor means materially destitute or without many of this world's goods. By application, or by the way Jesus uses it, He is talking about those who realize they are spiritually destitute, but are relying on God's righteousness through grace. Therefore, people who have **spiritual humility** will occupy the Kingdom of Heaven.

Remember, Heaven is gained not by our righteousness based on our merit, but rather by His righteousness based on His merit.

Who are the *persecuted for righteousness sake*? Jesus does not, in this passage, enlarge upon this category of persons. But, He will soon identify the **persecuted** as those who identify themselves with Him and suffer the hatred of the world with Him. You may be sure that when you choose to follow Christ as your Lord, the god of this world will bring his forces of evil against the Christ in you. Satan will test your commitment to Christ by making you—in some manner—pay for your commitment to Jesus. Our Lord says occupants of heaven are these types of people.

There has been an unnumbered list of believers who have stood the test of Satanic attack, and their faith never wavered. Beginning with the apostles, including those that suffered like Stephen and the saints who gave their lives in the coliseums of Rome, untold numbers have suffered for His testimony. Many continue in this present day to hold to an unwavering faith in the saving grace of God and His Son Jesus. These are among those who will occupy the kingdom of Heaven.

Jesus' sermon was not meant to include an exhaustive description of the residence of Heaven. We need to know, however, that the people in Heaven will all love holiness and righteousness. No one will be there that does not love God, and all He represents.

Jesus Taught:
Heaven is a Place for Stored Treasure

Matthew 6:19-21
19 Lay not up for yourselves treasures upon earth, where moth and rust doth corrupt, and where thieves break through and steal:
20 But lay up for yourselves treasures in heaven, where neither moth nor rust doth corrupt, and where thieves do not break through nor steal:
21 For where your treasure is, there will your heart be also.

179

Jesus taught spiritual concepts about Heaven that help us in our understanding. Our current consideration is an example. The idea that one can store spiritual treasures in Heaven without going there is ridiculous to the sophisticated modern mind. To speak in such a manner would be laughed to scorn in your average gathering of think-tankers whose minds had not been sanctified by the new birth. But, we who believe in Christ do not consider it strange at all.

When Christ called us, He did not ask us to abandon our minds, nor did He ask that we take a blind leap of faith. He asked us to consider the evidence that He has given us, and to make a choice of trust based on what He said in His Word. Remember, the rich man in Hell had asked Abraham to send Lazarus (the beggar) to warn his brothers about Hell, and Father Abraham (a hebraism for God) said if they will not hear Moses and the prophets, they would not believe one who had risen from the dead (Luke 16:27-31).

People believe what they choose to believe!

There are evidences for God's existence. Three of the most prominent are: (1) a material universe that is dependent on interrelated parts for continual existence (Romans 1:20); (2) the reality of a God consciousness and self-realization (John 1:9); (3) the intuitive knowledge of right and wrong (Romans 2:14). A man believes or rejects God based on the will of his own heart. No one has an excuse for not believing in God. God provides evidence for anyone who wants a reason to believe in Him (Romans 1:20).

Therefore, when Christ says that believers can build up treasures in Heaven, He is talking about an award system. The Father requires all to give an accounting for their acts, attitudes, thoughts, motives, and rebellions—including disobeying His standard of righteousness revealed in His Law. All Judgment is based on works whether we are sinners without Christ or sinners—God calls us saints— saved by grace (I Corinthians 3:13-15; Revelation 20:12). Therefore, all men must give an account of themselves to God. Then, at the appropriate time, all will be rewarded with degrees of punishment in Hell or degrees of blessings in Heaven.

Laying up treasure in Heaven not only applies to our positive response to the promptings of the Holy Spirit, but to our material investment of resources to further the causes of Christ. Things given now with the right motive are credited to our account in Heaven. If we do good things to be seen of men, then we have the reward now and credit will not be given in Heaven (Matthew 6:2). Be careful, do not do what you do to receive a reward! The motive behind our actions is revealing. Resolve in your heart to only glorify God with what you do or say.

Jesus Taught:
Heaven is a Prepared Place

John 14:1-3
1 Let not your heart be troubled: ye believe in
God, believe also in me.
2 In my Father's house are many mansions: if it
were not so, I would have told you. I go to prepare
a place for you.

3 And if I go and prepare a place for you, I will come again, and receive you unto myself; that where I am, there ye may be also.

After having told His hearers what kind of people will be in heaven, He now informs them that Heaven is being prepared for the arrival of His people. It is apparent from the text that there were those who were concerned about the afterlife. We are not given details about their concerns. However, Jesus makes several facts clear.

He first talks about the need for His hearers to trust Him in the way they have trusted His Father. He alleviates their fears by reassuring them of their inclusion. He also makes sure they know their eternity will be spent with Him.

The word mansions used by the translators would perhaps be better translated dwellings. It is not the idea of luxurious living that is being communicated, but rather an appropriate dwelling place conforming to an ambiance that brings glory to God. Whatever it looks like or feels like, it will have a "just right feeling." He goes on to say that it is especially prepared by Him for those who have placed their trust in Him.

Finally, He assures them that He will come again—just as He came the first time—and will receive them unto Himself. This is a personal assurance given to every hearer. No believer will be left behind. We are not told when this "coming again" will take place.

Bible students have deliberated over the possibilities of when He would return ever since His ascension from the Mount of Olives.

1. Some have taught that He was promising to come and take them to Heaven at their death.

2. Others believe He is describing an event that will take place at a general resurrection at the end of time.

3. Still others think that He is referencing a special time when He will come for the Church. (For a fuller explanation, see the chapter titled What Jesus Taught About the End Times.

Jesus Taught:
About a Vision of Heaven

When studying what Jesus taught, we must include not only the Gospels, but Jesus' revelation as spoken to His disciple John. Consider the vision recorded in Revelation Chapter 7.

Revelation 7:9-17
9 After this I beheld, and, lo, a great multitude, which no man could number, of all nations, and kindreds, and people, and tongues, stood before the throne, and before the Lamb, clothed with white robes, and palms in their hands;
10 And cried with a loud voice, saying, Salvation to our God which sitteth upon the throne, and unto the Lamb.
11 And all the angels stood round about the throne, and about the elders and the four beasts, and fell before the throne on their faces, and worshipped God,
12 Saying, Amen: Blessing, and glory, and wisdom, and thanksgiving, and honour, and power,

*and might, be unto our God for ever and ever.
Amen.*
*13 And one of the elders answered, saying unto
me, What are these which are arrayed in white
robes? and whence came they?*
*14 And I said unto him, Sir, thou knowest. And he
said to me, These are they which came out of great
tribulation, and have washed their robes, and
made them white in the blood of the Lamb.*
*15 Therefore are they before the throne of God,
and serve him day and night in his temple: and he
that sitteth on the throne shall dwell among them.*
*16 They shall hunger no more, neither thirst any
more; neither shall the sun light on them, nor any
heat.*
*17 For the Lamb which is in the midst of the
throne shall feed them, and shall lead them unto
living fountains of waters: and God shall wipe
away all tears from their eyes.*

In verse three of chapter seven John records that during the time of the end, angels are preparing to pour out wrath upon the earth. However, one angel declared: *Hurt not the earth, neither the sea, nor the trees, till we have sealed the servants of our God in their foreheads.* I believe this to be during the time of the **great tribulation** also known as **the time of Jacob's trouble** mentioned in verse fourteen of the above text. Then, John says those sealed will be one hundred and forty-four thousand. The number will consist of twelve thousand from each of the twelve tribes of Israel.

Then beginning with verse nine John sees another group of people who are arrayed in white robes. He is informed by the angel that these are the ones who will be saved during the tribulation. Most will have given their lives for the testimony of the Lord Jesus.

From the scene in Heaven that Jesus gave John, we learn some important information about what Heaven will be like.

(1) The attire of those in Heaven will be appropriate to their position as the redeemed of the Lord. Because we have inherited His righteousness, we will have attire that is white in color—depicting His holiness.

(2) While we are not given the nature of the service we are to render in Heaven, our purpose and goal will be to serve and please Him.

(3) The time of our service is everlasting. In eternity, the element of time does not exist. (We will no longer have a sin nature in Heaven, therefore, what ever service we are assigned, we will find joyous and refreshing. We will never grow weary in providing loving service to the glory of our Father and our Savior.)

(4) During time on earth believers suffered the plight of all mankind in that they suffered the pangs of thirst and hunger. In Heaven, the appetites of the flesh will no longer exist. Heat and cold will no longer be applicable. He will provide us with all needs by His very presence. We will enjoy the reality of glorified bodies. While in our present state, it is difficult to imagine a glorified state. The Gospel accounts give us some insight into what those bodies will be capable of by observing what Jesus did after His resurrection. For example, He could eat

and drink; He could appear and disappear; He had a physical body, He was not a ghost, for He invited Thomas to touch His crucifixion wounds; He had all His mental and emotional faculties. All Jesus' post resurrection experiences provide hints about what our eternal bodies will be like.

(5) John says in his account of the vision, that God will provide us with living fountains of water. The King will provide the needs of our heavenly state. We will be like God. However, in our heavenly state, we will have limitations. We will not be self-sustaining as is our God.

(6) John closes his account of the vision by declaring God shall wipe away all tears from their eyes. From John's vision we conclude that after God restores all the universe to its original state—a sinless universe, and concludes the final judgment on sin, all sorrow will be banned from existence. Hence, there will no longer be tears.

Finally, there is the Biblical statement recorded in Revelation 21:1-4 that deserves our attention.

> *Revelation 21:1-4*
> *1 And I saw a new heaven and a new earth: for the first heaven and the first earth were passed away; and there was no more sea.*
> *2 And I John saw the holy city, new Jerusalem, coming down from God out of heaven, prepared as a bride adorned for her husband.*
> *3 And I heard a great voice out of heaven saying, Behold, the tabernacle of God is with men, and he will dwell with them, and they shall be his people,*

*and God himself shall be with them, and be their
God.*
*4 And God shall wipe away all tears from their
eyes; and there shall be no more death, neither
sorrow, nor crying, neither shall there be any more
pain: for the former things are passed away.*

John's vision portrays a picture of new beginnings. He sees the earth as completely renewed. We are not told directly how the renewal will take place, but the implication is that it will be by fire. He even speaks of a new Heaven. We are not told why a new Heaven is needed nor is there a suggestion—only that a new Jerusalem will come down from the new Heaven.

Of all the things Jesus has taught about Heaven, the most important is—He will be there and we will experience ultimate fulfillment. We will soon embark on a great adventure that will never end.

Study Questions

1. What was the common concept of Heaven when Jesus entered His ministry?

2. Who does Jesus say dwells in Heaven?

3. What two characteristics will those have who occupy Heaven?

4. How does one store up treasure in Heaven?

5. What are some of the unique things that John revealed in his vision of Heaven?

6. Describe some of the things we learn about the glorified state from the resurrection appearances of Jesus.

CHAPTER 12

WHAT JESUS TAUGHT About the End Time

Because the Scriptures do not provide a chronological list of end-time events, we find ourselves searching His Word for hints and indicators to discover as much about these key events as possible. Godly men and women have disagreed through the centuries about how the end of our time on earth will finish.

Therefore, if you find yourself disagreeing with the presentation that follows, I ask you to practice tolerance. The Bible never makes doctrine about the end of time a test of fellowship. Christians should be willing to disagree agreeably over doctrines about the coming again of Christ. Our fellowship is in the person of Christ and His saving us—not by when He will come again.

The following observations come because of my understanding that the Word should be interpreted plainly or literally. I also recognize that the Bible uses symbolic and metaphorical language and should be interpreted as such when the context dictates. What I mean is—the context of the passage is to be used to explain its most likely meaning.

The Writer's Interpretation of What Jesus Taught About the End

Jesus' focus on the end of our age is taught most completely in one discourse. It is a summation of what really matters about the end of time. Because of the length of the passage, we will take a different approach from the one used in previous chapters.

As we take up the passage, remember, the Bible divides the world today into three groups of people: the Jews, the Gentiles, and the church of God (1 Corinthians 10:32). Jesus had alluded to the church, but thus far it had not been initiated. The church's founding began with the disciples being baptized by the Holy Spirit as recorded in Acts 2:1-4. (A Roman general destroyed the temple in 70 AD. By this time, the church had spread halfway around the known world.)

The most complete single passage about the end-times discussion is provided in Jesus' "Olivet Discourse" as recorded in The Gospel of Matthew. One must remember that what Jesus was teaching on that occasion was not a detailed chronological account of His coming, but a general overview.

Does that mean that we cannot take what He says at face value? No! It means that for understanding the details, we may have to depend on revelation supplied in other passages in both the Old and New Testaments. It is beyond the scope of our presentation to include all the Bible teaches about a particular subject.

The first question the disciples asked was: *When shall these things be*? It appears that the first question in the Matthew passage is addressed in Luke's account (Luke 21:20-24). One may well ask why? It is likely because Matthew presents Jesus as Messiah and the expected King, while Luke presents Him as the Servant of man. This is significant because when Jesus comes the second time, He will come as King and will set up His Kingdom. The destruction of Jerusalem and the temple as recorded in Matthew was already a reality.

We will begin this section with Luke's account of the predicted destruction of Jerusalem's temple.

Jesus Taught About:
The Destruction of Jerusalem

Luke 21:20-24
20 But when you see Jerusalem surrounded by armies, then know that its desolation has come near.
21 Then let those who are in Judea flee to the mountains, and let those who are inside the city

depart, and let not those who are out in the coun-
try enter it,
22 for these are days of vengeance, to fulfill all
that is written.
23 Alas for women who are pregnant and for
those who are nursing infants in those days! For
there will be great distress upon the earth and
wrath against this people.
24 They will fall by the edge of the sword and be
led captive among all nations, and Jerusalem will
be trampled underfoot by the Gentiles, until the
times of the Gentiles are fulfilled.

Jesus had just made an astounding prediction to His disciples about the destruction of the temple. It would be absolutely leveled with no stones left stacked. Some time after His prophecy, He and His disciples were resting on the Mount of Olives. The disciples might have assumed that Jesus' prediction was referring to the destruction at the end of the world. Or, they might have wanted to know time of the temple's destruction. Very much like us, the disciples wanted answers: When will it happen? What will be the signs?

Luke records the conditions that the people of Jerusalem will face during the attacks of the Roman legions: armies will circumvent the city; people will flee to the mountains; woman with pregnancies will be distressed; thousands will fall to the sword and others are taken into captivity; they trampled Jerusalem underfoot and occupied it until the times of the Gentiles are fulfilled. (The times of the Gentiles is a reference to God turning to the Gentile nations to offer them salvation through His Son.)

Since we believe the above prophecy has been fulfilled we can provide some historical information about what happened.

Some years after Jesus' ascension, several national leaders competed for the right to direct a revolt against Rome's tightfisted rule. Aware of the conflict in Judea, Rome sent Titus to quell the uprising. Jesus' prediction about the temple's destruction was fulfilled in 70 AD, when the Roman legions razed Jerusalem and utterly destroyed the temple. The Roman army, under Titus, destroyed the temple by fire. The fire was so intense that it caused the temple walls to crumble. It is reported that the rubble had to be sifted for melted gold.

The Luke passage describes perfectly the results of Titus' destruction of Jerusalem. The Jews were so badly beaten that most were either killed, captured, or fled to other nations. A hardcore remnant retreated to a mountain fortress at Masada located about thirty-five miles southeast of Jerusalem near En-gedi on the West side of the Dead Sea. Roman legions laid siege to the fortress for three years. In the end, it was an earthen ramp built by Jewish prisoners who were forced into service as slaves that allowed the capture of Masada. Josephus wrote that before the Roman soldiers entered, all but seven of the 960 Jews on Masada had committed mass suicide rather than be captured. The Roman victory was hollow. Thus, Jesus' prophecy of the temples destruction was fulfilled about seventy years after His ascension.

Jesus Taught About:
The Signs of His Second Coming

Be aware that Jesus' audience only consisted of His disciples who were Jews. Therefore, there would have been no reason to mention the church during His discourse. Why? Because, at that time, the church had not yet become a reality. Then, at the time of His second coming, the church will have been removed from the world. Therefore, there is no need for our Lord to include the church in the prophecy.

> *Matthew 24:3*
> *3 And as he sat upon the mount of Olives, the disciples came unto him privately, saying, Tell us, when shall these things be? and what shall be the sign of thy coming, and of the end of the world?*

Matthew's account provides insight into two issues (1) His second coming and (2) the end of the age. It is uncertain what the disciples were thinking. They might have thought the two events were immediately at hand. It is also possible His disciples thought the events were simultaneous. Regardless of what they were thinking, He answers their questions in the order of occurrence.

The phrase, Age of the Gentiles, is significant. It is the time when the Gentiles will be given predominate control of world affairs. Also, during this age God will call out of the Gentile nations a people for Himself. The age began with the ascension of Christ and will end when Christ calls out His church from the world (John 14:1-3; 1 Thessalonians 4:13-18). Be aware, the church will be made-up of all who believe in Christ from both Jewish and Gentile peoples. The primary apostle to the Gentiles was Paul. Soon after Paul was saved on the Damascus Road, Jesus taught him in the Arabian desert for three years (Galatians 1:15-18).

When Jesus comes again, the times of the Gentiles will close. That does not mean that Gentiles can no longer be saved. It only means that after the age, the Gentiles will not have God's evangelistic focus. For example, during this current age Jews may be saved but they do not appear to be God's focus. As a nation, the Jews are currently blinded spiritually (Romans 11:7).

Just prior to Christ's return anti-Semitism will intensify and God will awaken 144,000 Jews to the identification of Christ as their Messiah (Revelation 7:4-8). They will preach Christ and seek the salvation of souls everywhere. Just as the Gentile believers are evangelizing the world now, the Jewish evangelists will take up the glorious task during the great tribulation or the time of Jacob's trouble.

Jesus Taught About
Signs at the End of the Age

THE SIGN OF DECEPTION

Matthew 24 :4-5
4 And Jesus answered and said unto them, Take heed that no man deceive you.
5 For many shall come in my name, saying, I am Christ; and shall deceive many.

Jesus' first response is to warn them of widespread deception. Satan's forces will be frantic in their attempt to scuttle God's plans for final judgment. Deception is a major tool in his arsenal. An example of the deception might have been exemplified in the many false leaders that rose to lead Israel during the rebellious uprising against Rome. It is not a far stretch to believe that Satan engineered the whole affair in an attempt to destroy the Jews as he attempted to do again in World War II (Hitler's holocaust).

Satan will even energize some to falsely claim to be the Christ resulting in mass deception. There are many antichrists during this present age. However, during the great tribulation, there will finally arise a man who will be the personal embodiment of Satan who will be the Antichrist (Revelation 13:11-18).

Satan's deception is not unique to the great tribulation. Therefore, right now, we need to respond to Satanic deception by heeding John's warning to *try the spirits* (1 John 4:1). The spirit of a man may be tested by the truths provided in God's Word. Measuring everything by His truth is God's method of avoiding deception.

THE SIGN OF WAR

Jesus tells His disciples that during the great tribulation wars will still be rumored and waged.

> *Matthew 24:6-8*
> *6 And ye shall hear of wars and rumours of wars:*
> *see that ye be not troubled: for all these things*
> *must come to pass, but the end is not yet.*
> *7 For nation shall rise against nation, and king-*
> *dom against kingdom: and there shall be famines,*
> *and pestilences, and earthquakes, in divers places.*
> *8 All these are the beginning of sorrows.*

Jesus reminds His disciples that as long as sinful men roam the earth wars will continue until the millennial age of Christ's reign from Jerusalem (Revelation 21:1). Greed drives mankind to lust for domination. Such desires will continually ignite wars from generation to generation. It has been true since the days of Noah and according to Jesus; conditions of war will continue until His second coming. It has been approximately two thousand years since Christ's return to Heaven. Since then, we have had few years of world peace.

THE SIGN OF INTENSE PERSECUTION

Matthew 24:9-14
9 Then shall they deliver you up to be afflicted, and shall kill you: and ye shall be hated of all nations for my name's sake.
10 And then shall many be offended, and shall betray one another, and shall hate one another.
11 And many false prophets shall rise, and shall deceive many.
12 And because iniquity shall abound, the love of many shall wax cold.
13 But he that shall endure unto the end, the same shall be saved.
14 And this gospel of the kingdom shall be preached in all the world for a witness unto all nations; and then shall the end come.

In Matthew 24:9-14, we have the signs of **The Great Tribulation**. Remember, this is the time of intense persecution for all Jews and Gentiles who have come to believe on Christ after the catching away or rapture of the Church. As the Antichrist and his forces solidify their power, all

199

believers will be hunted down and summarily killed because they love Christ.

Jewish evangelists will preach the Gospel of the Kingdom to all the world. During this time love for God will wane and grow cold. False prophets will deceive many. The warning about false teachers and preachers applies to us today as much as it will then. The airways are filled with radio and television preachers and evangelists who are filling the minds of people with lies from Hell. There is only one Truth and that is the rightly understood Word of God. What does it mean to "rightly" understand the Word? It means that a person's understanding must be directed by the Holy Spirit.

THE SIGN OF TEMPLE DESECRATION

Sometime between now and the coming again of Christ, a Jewish temple will have to be built on the temple mount in Jerusalem—the very place where the Mosque of Omar currently rests. Rumors out of Israel indicate that plans are being drawn and priests are being trained for just such construction. We do not know if there is any truth in these rumors, but we do know that much research has gone into verifying the precise location of Herod's temple on the mount.

> *Matthew 24:15-22*
> *15 When ye therefore shall see the abomination of desolation, spoken of by Daniel the prophet, stand in the holy place, (whoso readeth, let him understand:)*
> *16 Then let them which be in Judaea flee into the mountains:*

17 Let him which is on the housetop not come down to take any thing out of his house:
18 Neither let him which is in the field return back to take his clothes.
19 And woe unto them that are with child, and to them that give suck in those days!
20 But pray ye that your flight be not in the winter, neither on the sabbath day:
21 For then shall be great tribulation, such as was not since the beginning of the world to this time, no, nor ever shall be.
22 And except those days should be shortened, there should no flesh be saved: but for the elect's sake those days shall be shortened.

Since 1948 Jews have been returning to Israel by the droves. They are immigrating from all over the world. A renewed spirit of anti-Semitism has driven them back to Israel. Could it be that our sovereign God is preparing our world for the fulfillment of His prophecy?

If the Bible is taken literally—before the Lord returns for the judgment of the nations after the battle at Armageddon—a temple will be in place in Jerusalem. During the great tribulation, the Antichrist will erect an image of himself in that temple. He will demand that he be worshipped. This act will be a desecration of God's holy place—an abomination to God.

Matthew 24:23-31
23 Then if any man shall say unto you, Lo, here is Christ, or there; believe it not.
24 For there shall arise false Christs, and false prophets, and shall shew great signs and wonders;

201

*insomuch that, if it were possible, they shall de-
ceive the very elect.*
25 Behold, I have told you before.
*26 Wherefore if they shall say unto you, Behold,
he is in the desert; go not forth: behold, he is in the
secret chambers; believe it not.*
*27 For as the lightning cometh out of the east,
and shineth even unto the west; so shall also the
coming of the Son of man be.*
*28 For wheresoever the carcase is, there will the
eagles be gathered together.*
*29 Immediately after the tribulation of those days
shall the sun be darkened, and the moon shall not
give her light, and the stars shall fall from heaven,
and the powers of the heavens shall be shaken:*
*30 And then shall appear the sign of the Son of
man in heaven: and then shall all the tribes of the
earth mourn, and they shall see the Son of man
coming in the clouds of heaven with power and
great glory.*
*31 And he shall send his angels with a great
sound of a trumpet, and they shall gather together
his elect from the four winds, from one end of
heaven to the other.*

Reports of the Lord's return will be everywhere, but they
are not to be believed. The sky will be filled with uncommon signs. Heavenly bodies will not appear normal. The
sky will look angry! When the Lord Jesus comes, He will
appear in the Eastern sky with His heavenly host.

End of Time Summary

Angels will gather those believers who survived the persecution of the great tribulation. The millennial reign will begin, and Satan will be chained in the bottomless pit. Near the end of Christ's reign in Jerusalem, Satan will be released for a final attempt at rebellion. The Devil will be defeated and cast into the lake of fire. The final judgment of the wicked will take place, fire will consume the world —God will provide a new heaven and a new earth. The new Jerusalem will come down from Heaven, and the people of God will begin a time of eternal worship, praise, and service.

My understanding of what the Bible teaches about the chronology of the endtimes follows. My theological position is technically pre-tribulation pre-millennialism: that means, I believe that Christ will rapture the church out of the world prior to the seven years of wrath that God will pour out on the world prior to Christ's thousand years of reign on earth. As I understand it, the ordered events will be as follows.

1. The Church—the bride of Christ—whose names are in the book of life—is currently in process (Ephesians 1:3-6);

2. At an unannounced time Christ will call His Church out of the world into heaven. (1 Thessalonians 4:13-18; John 14:1-3; 1Corinthians 15:51-58);

3. At the catching-up or rapture of the church, a period of "Great Tribulation" will commence. (It is a period of wrath from God on evil in the world. See its characteristics in Matthew 24:21 and Revelation 6:15-17;

4.   At the conclusion of the seven-year tribulation, Christ will come with His angels to do battle with the kingdoms of this world under the direction of the Antichrist (Revelation 19:6);

5. The angels of the Lord will gather those saved during the tribulation, and they will enter the millennium to enjoy the reign of Christ their King;

6. The angels will gather the lost peoples of the world for the judgment of the nations (Matthew 25:31-46; Joel 3:2);

7. Christ will establish His kingdom in Jerusalem and will rule the world from there for a thousand years;

8. The bottomless pit is Satan's prison until the end of the thousand years (Revelation 20:1-3);

9.   Near the end of the thousand years, Satan will be released to lead a final assault on Christ (Revelation 20:7-9);

10. Christ will squelch the revolt and cast all participants with Satan and his fallen angels in the Lake of Fire (Revelation 20:10);

11. The remaining resurrected dead are judged—assigned punishment according to their works and cast into the Lake of Fire (Revelation 20:11-15); and

12. The people of God will have a New Heaven and the New Earth and will launch a sinless environment as they spend their eternity in praise of God and His Son in the power of His Spirit (Revelation 21:1-22:5).

BRIEF SUMMARY OF VARIOUS END TIMES INTERPRETATIONS

POST-MILLENNIALISM

Christians who adopt this view believe that Christ will return after the millennium. The work of the gospel on earth will lead to a thousand years of man living in social harmony having resolved his human ills. The church will usher in an unheard-of achievement of millennial peace prior to Christ's return.

A-MILLENNIALISM

The prefix "A" in Latin is a negative; therefore, this viewpoint teaches that there will not be a literal millennial reign of Christ. Whatever kingdom there is, is now—it is heaven's present rule over the church. They believe that Israel was the church in the Old Testament and that God abandoned Israel as a nation—because of their disobedience. Adherents say he church is the new spiritual Israel. Conditions in this present age will become increasingly worse until the second advent of Christ. At the return of the Lord, there is a second resurrection and judgment followed by eternity.

The church, in the A-millennial interpretation, fulfills the promises made to Israel. According to this view, Revelation 20 describes the scene of souls in heaven between the first and second comings of Christ.

HISTORIC PRE-MILLENNIALISM

The pre-millennial position holds that the second coming of Christ will occur before the thousand years. Christ will establish His kingdom in Jerusalem and physically reign over the earth as King. During the millennium, the Jewish people will experience the fulfillment of the covenants made to Abraham and David.

Pre-millennialism believes the present church period will see increasing apostasy until the time of "great" tribulation (It is a time of intense suffering when God unleashes His plaques of wrath upon the wicked for seven years). Then, at the end of the tribulation period, we will see the literal second coming of Christ to the earth. When He triumphantly returns, He will set up His kingdom for a thousand years. When His reign is finished, He will call for a resurrection of the dead and will pronounce their judgment. He will usher in a sinless eternity.

Pre-millennialism interprets the covenants and prophecies of Scripture plainly.

(Some in this group believe the church will go through the tribulation but God will provide protection like unto Noah and his family during the flood.)

PRE-TRIBULATION & MID-TRIBULATION PRE-MILLENNIALISM

Christians taking this position believe that Christ will rapture, or catch up, His church to heaven prior to the seven years of God's judgment predicted by the books of Daniel and Revelation. The prefix "pre" means before; hence, we have "pre-tribulation" or before the tribulation.

Some take a mid-tribulation position believing that the church will go through the first three and one-half years and then be raptured.

There are several interpretative variables within the pre-tribulation school of thought.

A Final Word

The ultimate message of the end-time is that man is accountable to God who is Holy and deserving of worship. Everyone will live somewhere forever. Where we spend our eternity will depend on how we have responded to Jesus Christ—God's Son.

Remember these few things that the vast majority of Bible believer's accept:

1. Christ will come a second time—making a literal appearance.

2. His coming will be followed by judgment. (No one will escape being accountable to God for how they have lived their lives. The actions of our lives do not determine our destination, only the reward, or punishment. Salvation is determined by how we have responded to Christ.)

3. Those who have (in faith) received Christ will enter the realization of their glorified state and live in the blissful presence of God forever.

4. Those who have not received Christ will be cast into the lake of fire and will spend their eternity in torment prepared for the Devil and his fallen angels.

Study Questions

1. What is meant by the term "second coming?"

2. What is meant by the term a-millennial?

3. What is meant by post-millennial?

4. What is meant by pre-millennial?

5. What is meant by pre-tribulation?

6. What end-time position do you hold and why?

Parables of Christ

Wise and foolish builders	Matthew 7:24–27
Bride-chamber Children	Matthew 9:15
New cloth & old garment	Matthew 9:16
New wine & old bottles	Matthew 9:17.
Unclean spirit	Matthew 12:43.
Sower	Matthew 13:3, 18
	Luke 8:5, 11
Tares	Matthew 13:24–30, 36–43
Mustard seed	Matthew 13:31, 32.
	Luke 13:19
Leaven	Matthew 13:33.
Treasure hid in a field	Matthew 13:44.
Pearl of great price	Matthew 13:45, 46.
Net cast into the sea	Matthew 13:47–50
Meats defiling not	Matthew 15:10–15
Unmerciful servant	Matthew 18:23–35
Laborers hired	Matthew 20:1–16
Two sons	Matthew 21:28–32
Wicked husbandmen	Matthew. 21:33–45
Marriage feast	Matthew 22:2–14
Fig-tree leafing	Matthew 24:32–34

Man of the house watching	Matthew 24:43
Faithful & evil servants	Matthew 24:45–51
Ten virgins	Matthew 25:1–13
Talents	Matthew 25:14–30
Divided kingdom	Mark 3:24
House divided	Mark 3:25
Strong man armed	Mark 3:27
	Luke 11:21.
Seed growing secretly	Mark 4:26–29
Lighted candle	Mark 4:21
	Luke 11:33–36
Man taking a far journey	Mark 13:34–37
Blind leading the blind	Luke 6:39.
Beam and mote	Luke 6:41, 42.
Tree and its fruit	Luke 6:43–45
Creditor and debtors	Luke 7:41–47
Good Samaritan	Luke 10:30–37
Importunate friend	Luke 11:5–9
Rich fool	Luke 12:16–21.
Cloud and wind	Luke 12:54–57.
Barren fig-tree	Luke 13:6–9.
Men bidden to a feast	Luke 14:7–11
Builder of a tower	Luke 14:28–30,33

King going to war	Luke 14:31–33
Savor of salt	Luke 14:34, 35
Lost sheep	Luke 15:3–7
Lost piece of silver	Luke 15:8–10.
Prodigal son	Luke 15:11–32
Unjust steward	Luke 16:1–8
Rich man and Lazarus	Luke 16:19–31
Importunate widow	Luke 18:1–8
Pharisee and Publican	Luke 18:9–14
Pounds	Luke 19:12–27
Good Shepherd	John 10:1–6
Vine and branches	John 15:1–5

The Miracles of Christ

Water turned to wine	John 2:6–10.
Nobleman's son healed	John 4:46–53.
Centurion's servant healed	Matthew 9:5–13.
Draughts of fish.	Luke 5:4–6; John 21:6
Devils cast out	Matthew 8:28–32
	Matthew 9:32, 33;
	Matthew15:22–28;
	Matthew 17:14–18;
	Mark 1:23–27
Peter's wife's mother	Matthew 8:14, 15
Lepers cleansed	Matthew 8:3; Luke 17:14
Paralytic healed	Mark 2:3–12.
Withered hand restored	Matthew 12:10–13.
Impotent man healed	John 5:5–9
The dead raised to life	Matthew 9:18; Matthew 19:23–25; Luke 7:12–15; John 11:11–44
Issue of blood stopped	Matthew 9:20–22.

The blind restored to sight	Matthew 9:27–30; Mark 8:22–25; John 9:1–7
The deaf and dumb cured	Mark 7:32–35.
The multitude fed	Matthew 14:15–21; Matthew 15:32–38
His walking on the sea	Matthew 14:25–27
Peter walking on the sea	Matthew 14:29.
Tempest stilled	Matthew 8:23–26;14:32
Sudden arrival of the ship	John 6:21
Tribute money	Matthew 17:27
Woman healed of infirmity	Luke 13:11–13
Dropsy cured	Luke 14:2–4
Fig tree blighted	Matthew 21:19.
Malchus healed	Luke 22:50, 51.
Performed before the messengers of John	Luke 7:21, 22.
Many and divers diseases healed	Matthew 4:23, 24; Matthew 14:14; Matthew15:30; Mark 1:34; Luke 6:17–19
His transfiguration	Matthew 17:1–8
His resurrection	Luke 24:6; John 10:18

His appearance to his disciples, the doors being shut.

John 20:19

His ascension   Acts 1:9

222 PLAN PUBLICATIONS

By William L. Owens available from

The 222 Plan Manual will guide a mentor in the process of building Christian disciplines into the life of another. Based on 2 Timothy 2:2, it is God's plan for making disciples. For information on

The Christian is engaged in spiritual warfare with Satan and the forces of evil. If you want to be more informed about this conflict and how to deal with the enemy of

Jesus taught His disciples about key issues that hat eternal implications. These issues are still relevant for the twenty-first century. Read this book and you will know what Jesus' disciples learned.

When Jesus called Paul aside into Arabia, He taught Him things hidden by God from the foundations of the world. These "secrets" or mysteries are shared and

Made in the USA
Columbia, SC
09 December 2018